Montessori Topics of Interest

Mary Da Prato, AMI Diploma

CreateSpace Independent Publishing Platform
Copyright © 2018 Mary Da Prato
All rights reserved.

ISBN: 1717383270
ISBN-13: 978-1717383273

Mary Da Prato

ACKNOWLEDGMENTS

The article "Beyond the Pink Tower: What Parents Need to Know about the Primary Montessori Prepared Environment" was originally published in *Montessori Pro Rodinu*, a Czech parent magazine, January 2014. The Czech article can be viewed at: http://www.montessoridoma.cz/wp-content/uploads/downloads/2014/02/montessori-pro-rodinu-leden-2014-emailing.pdf.

Mary Da Prato

DISCLAIMERS

In this publication, parents, guides, and assistants are referred to as "she," while students are called "he." These designations, assigned for the reader's convenience, are in no way intended to reflect the gender dynamic of parents, teachers, and students in a Montessori environment.

Children in the Montessori prepared environment are supervised at all times for safety. Be sure to supervise your child when working with any small activity pieces which can be a choking hazard. Put all small pieces out of the reach of children when not in use.

TABLE OF CONTENTS

Mary Da Prato

INTRODUCTION

What Is Montessori?

The Montessori Method of education, developed by Dr. Maria Montessori in 1907, emphasizes freedom of movement and work choice in a mixed-age classroom during a three hour uninterrupted time block under the guidance of a trained Montessori teacher in accordance with universal laws of human development. For more than one hundred years on every inhabited continent, Montessori's scientific and humanitarian pedagogy of guiding each individual child to his fullest potential has endured.

Dr. Montessori founded Association Montessori Internationale (AMI) in 1929 to preserve the high standards of her scientific method. This publication reflects the author's AMI Primary training. There are other Montessori training courses including AMS (American Montessori Society), PAMS (Pan American Montessori Society), and St. Nicholas Montessori, but this publication focuses on the original Montessori Method of education as founded by Dr. Maria Montessori herself as presented to the author via oral tradition by an AMI teacher trainer.

For more information about the Montessori Method, consult the writings of Dr. Maria Montessori as well as contemporary titles including *Montessori for You and Your Child* by Mary Da Prato.

About this Book

Montessori Topics of Interest is a collection of ten essays about various aspects of the Montessori Primary prepared environment's philosophy and pedagogy. Each essay explores a particular Montessori topic for the benefit of parents, educators, and anyone interested in learning more about Montessori. References are provided at the end of each article for further research. Enjoy!

BEYOND THE PINK TOWER: WHAT PARENTS NEED TO KNOW ABOUT THE PRIMARY MONTESSORI PREPARED ENVIRONMENT

A Montessori Casa, or classroom for three to six year old students, consists of three core elements: developmentally appropriate mixed-age groups, the trained Montessori guide, and a complete set of the official scientifically designed Montessori manipulatives.[1] The combination of these three essential elements becomes the Prepared Environment, a learning environment that best suits the physical, intellectual, and emotional development of each individual child. For optimal results, Montessori students are organized into three year mixed-age groups instead of single-age groups. The appropriate three year age groupings are determined by stages of cognitive development known in Montessori as the "Four Planes of Development." Children from birth through six years of age comprise the First Plane. The First Plane can be divided into two age groups: birth through three years of age and three through six years of age. A Montessori Casa dei Bambini, or Children's House, is designed to best meet the needs and desires of children ages three through six, although many students are ready to begin their life in the Casa at two years and ten months of age depending on readiness. In a mixed-age environment, younger students have older children, not just adults, as friends, mentors, and advocates. Older children in turn have the opportunity to assist their younger peers which reinforces self-esteem, patience, and compassion. Additionally, older children gain confidence in their own skills by helping their younger classmates. An older child who helps a younger child tie a bow, for example, refines his own bow tying skills.

---

[1] Montessori, Maria. *The Secret of Childhood*. Trans. Barbara B. Carter. Hyderabad: Orient Longman, 2006. Print. Page 147.

To further support social skills among mixed-age groups of children, and to ensure the correct proportion of three, four, five, and six year olds in a given Casa, twenty-five to forty students should be in a single classroom with only one teacher and as many aides as are required for supervision purposes. Contrary to popular belief, small class sizes make students too dependent upon adult assistance, which eliminates the opportunity to develop individual problem solving skills. Classes with too few students also limit social interactions among different ages of children within the Casa. A small class of ten students, for instance, may only have one or two five year olds whereas a class of forty students would likely have ten five year olds to interact with and assist younger students.

Despite relatively large class sizes, students in a Montessori Casa receive much one-on-one attention from the trained Montessori teacher in the form of individual or small group lessons known as presentations. Unlike a traditional teacher who acts as a lecturer in front of the entire class, a Montessori teacher guides individual students through developmentally appropriate presentations in various sequential skills at the child's pace. The length of a presentation depends upon its complexity and the student's understanding of the material. Once the lesson is complete, the guide gives control of the manipulative to the child and retreats to the perimeter of the room to observe. Now that the child has received the material's initial presentation, he is free to use the manipulative for as long as he wishes or put it away to use at another time. Either way, the child no longer needs the guide to assist him with the material presented because the material itself will teach him from this moment forward. It is not even necessary for the guide to correct the child's work with the manipulative because of its self-correcting nature known as the "control of error." Work with a didactic manipulative such as the Cylinder Blocks, for example, is very straightforward even to the youngest students. In this exercise, there are ten precisely measured cylinders which must be placed into the correct holes of the Cylinder Block. If the child places a cylinder in the incorrect hole, it will not fit properly. The guide does not need to correct the child because the control of error, in this case the cylinder not fitting in the hole, is perfectly obvious. The control of error allows the child to independently correct his own mistakes without the embarrassment that comes from traditional corrections such as bad grades and red marks on a paper. Through self-correction, however, students develop friendliness toward error which allows them the freedom to make mistakes and to learn from them without external pressure or guidance. Students have ample time to repeat tasks, correct mistakes, and make discoveries because they choose their own work during an uninterrupted three hour time block.

In the child-centered Prepared Environment, children are free to choose their own work within natural limits. Starting on the first day of school, new students are familiarized with the three main rules of the Casa. First, any child may take a material he has had a lesson in from the shelf. Second, the child who takes the material may use it for as long as he wants. Third, when he is done using the material, he must return it to the proper place on the shelf in its original condition. These three simple rules regarding classroom procedures eliminate the need to create long lists of behavioral expectations in the Casa. The first rule, which states that any child may take a material he has had a lesson in from the shelf, establishes order in self-directed learning. If a material is not on the shelf, that material is not allowed to be taken away from the child who is currently using it. This rule protects a child who is working from intrusion by other students and even other adults in the room. As long as a child is using a material properly during work time, not even the teacher may interrupt him or tell him he must share the manipulative with another child. If the child were forced to share, it would disrupt his concentration and the ability to use the material to its best advantage as most manipulatives are designed for individual use. To disrupt the child would also be a violation of the second rule of the classroom, which states that a child who has taken a material from the shelf may work with that material for as long as he wants. Once the material is returned to the shelf in its original condition, any child who has had a lesson may take it and use it, which satisfies the third rule of the classroom. This is a more natural way for young children to share and helps develop patience and problem solving skills. Since there is only one of each material in the classroom, and a child may not take an unavailable material from another child, he must decide independently what he would like to do while waiting to use the manipulative of his choice.

Freedom of choice extends beyond the Primary classroom's didactic materials. Children in the Casa are also free to choose when they would like to use the restroom, drink water, or eat a snack. To preserve and protect each child's dignity and to promote functional independence, none of these actions require permission from an adult. The organization of the Prepared Environment itself allows children to safely perform these tasks independently. A bathroom, drinking fountain or water cooler, and snack preparation materials are located within the Casa for ease of use. Many Prepared Environments also include a fenced outdoor environment adjacent to the Casa which children may access at will during work time provided they are dressed appropriately for the weather. The outdoor environment, or outdoor classroom, is just as educational as the indoor classroom. Outdoor experiences such as gardening and botany are both educational fields best learned outdoors. Traditional childhood games like hide and seek, tag, and jump rope promote physical fitness as well as the opportunity to take turns and otherwise get along with one another. On pleasant days, activities from the classroom such as reading, painting, and geography puzzles, can be taken to tables that are located outside so that children can enjoy the fresh air while they work.[2][3]

Montessori materials and activities are organized into four areas of focus: Practical Life, Sensorial, Language, and Mathematics. Practical Life activities are the child's entry point into the classroom. Games and exercises that promote gross and fine motor coordination, manners, hygiene, personal care, environmental care, and art are all included in this area. [4] [5] Children learn values such as respect, cooperation, taking turns, and peaceful conflict resolution through brief skits called "Grace and Courtesy" or "Social Relations." These lessons are performed by the teacher who is sometimes assisted by the aide and older children.[6] Fun activities such as "Walking on the Line" give children the opportunity to improve balance and motor skills. "Care of the Person" activities include practical exercises such as "Dressing Frames" that help children practice buttoning buttons and tying bows. Through "Care of the Environment," students learn how to care for clothing, plants, animals, and any other aspects of the environment that need attention.[7]

Sensorial materials are used to explore the five senses and their qualities. There is an activity for each sense: touch, visual, auditory, smell, and taste. The qualities of a sense, such as color, texture, and pitch, are also explored in separate materials.[8] When a child has ample experience with each isolated Sensorial exercise,

---

[2] Montessori, Maria. "The House of Children." *The NAMTA Journal* 38.1 (2013): 11-19. Print.

[3] Montessori, Maria. "Nature in Education." *The NAMTA Journal* 38.1 (2013): 21-27. Print.

[4] Montessori, Maria. *The Discovery of the Child*. Trans. Mary A. Johnstone. Chennai: Kalakshetra, 2006. Print. Pages 86-88.

[5] Montessori, Maria. *Dr. Montessori's Own Handbook*. Mineola: Dover Publications, 2005. Print. Pages 18-30.

[6] Montessori, Maria. *The Secret of Childhood*. Trans. Barbara B. Carter. Hyderabad: Orient Longman, 2006. Print. Pages 132-135.

[7] Montessori, Maria. *Dr. Montessori's Own Handbook*. Mineola: Dover Publications, 2005. Print. Pages 18-30.

[8] Ibid. Pages 30-87.

he will be given lessons in "Mixed Impression" activities. Mixed Impression materials use combinations of the senses that the child has already experienced. Geography and Botany are also classified as Sensorial exercises because of how they are used. Materials such as the Sandpaper Globe and Painted Globe provide a concrete, tactile introduction to the abstract world of Geography. Continents and countries are represented by removable puzzle pieces on a map. Leaf shapes in the botany area are also presented as puzzle pieces that the child can manipulate, trace, and identify.

Formal and informal language exercises are integral to the Montessori curriculum on both an academic and social level. Structured academic language activities include vocabulary lessons, writing, reading, spelling, and sentence diagramming. All of these lessons are presented in a developmentally appropriate manner that children also find enjoyable. In addition to these individual presentations, children have the opportunity to participate in group activities that focus on spoken language. At any time of the day, adults in the room may initiate spoken language experiences such as reading books, telling oral stories, reading poetry, singing songs, and playing games such as "I Spy" with children who are interested. Listening to stories and playing language games are not only entertaining but enrich vocabulary and prepare the child for creative writing in the future.[9] Fun with language extends beyond the academic and into the social realm. Children in the Casa learn how to interact with one another respectfully and are free to do so at almost any time. Casual conversations between children and adults or children and other children help students perfect their spoken language skills and the art of conversation. Conversation is considered a legitimate work choice for children in the Casa and is as respected as all other subject areas.[10]

---

[9] Ibid. Pages 91-109.
[10] Montessori, Maria. *The Absorbent Mind*. Vol. 1. Oxford: Clio, 2004. Print. The Clio Montessori Ser. Pages 111-112.

The study of mathematics begins when a child is about four years old, although an individual child may be ready for his first math lesson sooner or later than the suggested age. Math exercises in the Casa include manipulating numbers through the millions; exploring the four operations of addition, subtraction, multiplication, and division; solving word problems; and working with fractions. It is important to note that these math experiences are not burdensome since they are presented when developmentally appropriate using concrete manipulatives and games that are naturally attractive to children.[11]

Subjects such as art, botany, drama, geography, and music used to belong to an area of focus called "Cultural Extensions," but are now woven into the other four areas of the Casa. Cultural Extension exercises are incorporated into the other subject areas to prevent them from being considered superfluous when they are, in fact, just as essential to the holistic development of the individual child as practical skills and academics. The guide is responsible for presenting every lesson in each subject area, including activities such as art and music. There are no separate art or music teachers in the Casa because art and music are integrated within the holistic framework of the Casa. Just like any other presentation, students are free to choose art and music exercises at will during their uninterrupted three hour time block following an initial presentation. Above all, every lesson in the Casa is fun, open-ended, and cognitively suitable for three to six year old children.

Besides mixed-age groups, a trained Montessori guide, and didactic materials, the Prepared Environment also relies upon parental involvement. Parents and the Montessori guide form a partnership that is essential to each child's education. Being an effective Montessori parent extends beyond attendance at parent-

---

[11] Montessori, Maria. *Creative Development in the Child.* Ed. Rukmini Ramachandran. Vol. 1. Chennai: Kalakshetra, 1998. Print. Pages 132-134.

teacher conferences, parent nights, and other school functions. Montessori is a lifestyle. The Prepared Environment children experience in the Casa should be reinforced at home. Even if you are not Montessori trained, there are small ways you can bring Montessori into your home. Begin with simple accommodations such as providing your children with open shelving for their activities rather than tossing articles into a disorganized toy chest. Provide your child with a child-sized rug as a work and play space that controls clutter. Have intelligent conversations with your child about age-appropriate topics such as nature in their backyard or in the park. Involve your child and encourage participation in age-appropriate household tasks under adult supervision such as folding laundry, matching socks, assisting in feeding pets, and measuring dry and liquid ingredients during meal preparation. When you attend your next parent-teacher conference, ask your child's guide for additional ideas on how to make your home Montessori friendly and child-centered. Creating a Prepared Environment at home is not necessarily an easy task, but it is a worthwhile task, one that prepares children for life.

References

Montessori, Maria. *The Absorbent Mind*. Vol. 1. Oxford: Clio, 2004. Print. The Clio Montessori Ser.

Montessori, Maria. *Creative Development in the Child*. Ed. Rukmini Ramachandran. Vol. 1. Chennai: Kalakshetra, 1998. Print.

Montessori, Maria. *The Discovery of the Child*. Trans. Mary A. Johnstone. Chennai: Kalakshetra, 2006. Print.

Montessori, Maria. *Dr. Montessori's Own Handbook*. Mineola: Dover Publications, 2005. Print

Montessori, Maria. "The House of Children." *The NAMTA Journal* 38.1 (2013): 11-19. Print.

Montessori, Maria. "Nature in Education." *The NAMTA Journal* 38.1 (2013): 21-27. Print.

Montessori, Maria. *The Secret of Childhood*. Trans. Barbara B. Carter. Hyderabad: Orient Longman, 2006. Print.

Mary Da Prato

MONTESSORI PRIMARY EDUCATION: RATIONAL, NOT RIGID

An often heard criticism of Montessori Primary education is that the curriculum is too rigid or obsessed with making students follow a strict sequence of actions in order to perform any given task. The Montessori Method is too stifling, some critics say, and squashes creativity through its regimentation. As Montessorians, we know this description is a gross misrepresentation of our child-centered prepared environments. Unfortunately, mainstream misunderstanding of our pedagogy is pervasive. Is Montessori Primary education structured? Of course. Is it rigid and regimented? Of course not! What many in the mainstream fail to realize is that Montessori education embodies an appropriate balance between student freedom of work choice and the rational limits placed upon work that students have chosen freely. Let's look at the presentation "Washing a Table" as an example.

When a child chooses Washing a Table as an independent work choice during the Casa's uninterrupted work period, he may select any available child-sized table to wash. "Any available table" means one that is not currently occupied by a student or manipulatives. Naturally, the student may not choose a table where another student is working as this would constitute a violation of personal space as well as other logistical problems. In this situation, the child who wants to wash a table that is currently unavailable is confronted with a rational restriction. Since the table is occupied, he must wait until it is available or choose a different table to wash. This promotes spontaneous problem solving skills as the student must ultimately decide what to do within the natural limits of the Casa. The policy of not permitting a student to wash an occupied table can hardly be called rigid or regimented. It is simply common sense.

Very well, critics may say, but what about when the child

actually begins to wash the available table of his choice? Is he not compelled to wash the table using an exact, prescribed, non-negotiable sequence of actions dictated by the guide? Let us examine this concern in detail. To begin, it is absolutely true that Washing a Table is performed using a specific, ordered sequence of actions. But this is not because the guide is being overly particular or tyrannical. Rather, the logical sequence of actions required during Washing a Table is dictated by the restrictions of the manipulative itself![12] Once the child has gathered the Washing a Table materials and placed them beside his chosen table, he must fill the provided pitcher with water. This is a necessary first step in the activity as Washing a Table is impossible without first retrieving water for washing. Again, it is not the guide who demands that the child fill the pitcher with water before taking further action, but the rational restraints of the activity itself.

When the child returns with the pitcher of water, he pours about a third of its contents into a basin. Only a third of the water is poured into the basin at this time as the other two-thirds will be needed later during the exercise. In the meantime, the pitcher of water is set aside. The child then submerges a sponge in the basin. As soon as the sponge is saturated with water, the child removes it from the basin and washes the table using a zigzag motion. First, he wipes the table from left to right, top to bottom to remove dust. Next, using the same zigzag motion, the child wipes the table from top to bottom, left to right. Outside of the Montessori community, this sequence of events may appear arbitrary and nonsensical. After all, what difference does it make if the child wipes from left to right or right to left? Who cares if the child makes a zigzag motion? As long as the table gets clean, what difference does it make whether the child follows the prescribed table washing pattern or not? But this mainstream interpretation of Washing a

---

[12] Montessori, Maria. *Creative Development in the Child.* Ed. Rukmini Ramachandran. Vol. 1. Chennai: Kalakshetra, 2007. Print. Pages 52-60.

Table is a misconception. When a child washes the table using a zigzag motion, first horizontally from left to right, top to bottom, and then vertically from top to bottom, left to right, he is not doing so for the mere purpose of washing the table. In fact, a young child probably does not care whether the table becomes clean or not![13] Like all Practical Life activities in the Casa, the pattern of the activity is designed to promote and improve the child's gross motor and fine motor coordination. The broad zigzag motion across the table's surface not only ensures that the table will become clean, it also exercises the child's dominant arm in preparation for writing in the future. By wiping the table from left to right, the child's eyes are prepared for tracking in that direction, the same direction in which we read and write the English language. Rather than being a burden, these precise motions are naturally appealing to young children, particularly those under four-and-a-half years of age, due to their Sensitive Periods for order, movement, and refinement of sensory perception.[14] The young child is not particularly interested in the table itself. Instead, he is intensely motivated to clean the table using a precise sequence of actions in order to satisfy his inner directive to improve his gross and fine motor control.[15] It is for this reason that the Montessori Primary guide prepares an environment filled with opportunities for the child to exercise his gross motor coordination and improve his fine motor control in a precise fashion that is naturally appealing.[16]

After wiping the table with the wet sponge, the child scrubs the table from left to right, top to bottom with a soapy scrub brush. Instead of making zigzag motions as he did with the sponge, the child makes small circular motions with the scrub brush across the surface of the table from left to right. Slow motions are used near

---

[13] Ibid. Pages 52-59.

[14] Ibid. Pages 52-63, 89-101.

[15] Ibid. Pages 52-59.

[16] Ibid.

the edges of the table to prevent splashing and improve coordination. Fast, vigorous motions are used when scrubbing the middle of the table to strengthen the dominant hand for writing in the future. Every movement performed during Washing a Table, whether slow or fast, is designed to best meet young children's innate developmental needs and tendencies toward gross coordination development and refinement of fine motor control.[17]

When the child is finished scrubbing the table with the scrub brush, it is necessary to remove the soap residue from the table. To do this, the child uses the sponge, repeating the zigzag motions he performed earlier in the exercise. As soap accumulates on the wet sponge, it becomes necessary to wash the sponge in the basin and then lightly wring it out before continuing. If the sponge is too soapy, it will spread soap around the surface of the table rather than removing it. This observation generally does not require the guide's assistance following the initial presentation. The sponge itself indicates when it is time to be cleaned.

Once the task of wiping away soap suds with the sponge is complete, the child empties the soapy water from the basin into a designated location in the Casa. Upon return, he refills the basin with half of the water remaining in the pitcher. The sponge is then submerged in the clean water, wrung out, and then used to wipe the table to remove any remaining soap residue. To clean the table, the child first wipes horizontally from left to right, top to bottom. He then wipes vertically from top to bottom, left to right. Next, he wipes the around the perimeter of the table to remove any remaining soap that may have clung to the table's edges.

Finally, the child dries the table with a towel using the familiar zigzag motion from left to right, top to bottom, followed by top to bottom, left to right. After cleaning up any additional drips, the child empties the basin in a designated location. The remaining water in the pitcher is poured into the basin to wash away any soap

---

[17] Ibid.

residue. Once again, the basin is emptied in a designated location. Any drips in the work area are wiped up with the towel. When the area is clean and dry, the Washing a Table exercise is returned to its proper location in the Casa in its original condition. The activity is then complete, and the child is free to choose other work.

You will notice that throughout the long process of Washing a Table, there is not a single arbitrary or superfluous step. The alleged rigidity of the exercise is nothing more than the natural and logical sequence of actions required to complete the task in the most reasonable manner possible while simultaneously fulfilling the child's developmental needs for order, movement, and refinement of sensory perception. By following the rational sequence for Washing a Table originally demonstrated by the guide, the child is not only able to complete the task successfully but is prepared for increasingly advanced work in the future. A child who can follow an exact sequence during Washing a Table and other Practical Life exercises has been provided with a solid foundation for following the precise steps needed to complete complex academic tasks including solving mathematics equations.[18]

If the example of Washing a Table is not enough to convince critics of the vital importance of completing work which follows a logical sequence, consider the necessity of taking precise steps when solving a mathematics equation. In mathematics, following the prescribed order of operations is non-negotiable when solving equations. The specific sequence in which equations must be solved is as follows: parentheses, exponents, multiplication, division, addition, and subtraction. To aid memory, the correct order of operations is often assigned the mnemonic "Please Excuse My Dear Aunt Sally," a sentence which may be familiar from grade school or high school. Whether or not a mnemonic is used, the order of operations must be followed to discover the correct

---

[18] Montessori, Maria. *Dr. Montessori's Own Handbook*. Mineola: Dover Publications, 2005. Print. Pages 91-94, 116-117.

answer. In our increasingly academic world, the exactitude of mathematics is common knowledge that all students are eventually expected to know. But would anyone accuse the order of operations, or mathematics in general, of being too rigid? In a fashion, the subject of mathematics fits many Montessori critics' accusation of rigidity, the claim that each task must be completed in a certain, specified, sequential manner. On the surface, the accusation appears to be correct. Whether in a Montessori classroom or elsewhere, there is no opinion or interpretation when it comes to solving a mathematical equation. The answer is either correct or incorrect. This is a fact not often questioned in the realm of mathematics. There is, however, often harsh criticism of the sequential nature of Montessori manipulatives outside of mathematics. But just as a mathematical equation must be solved in a certain manner in order to achieve the answer, Washing a Table must be completed in a particular fashion in order to achieve the desired result. Just as exponential expressions must be solved before addition within a mathematics equation, a table must be washed with a damp sponge before soap is added during Washing a Table. Performing given tasks in a specified order is not tyranny but rationality.

The logical sequences in which various manipulatives and tasks are presented follow a natural progression. In both Montessori and traditional education, addition is taught before multiplication. This makes absolute sense because multiplication is the same quantity added to itself multiple times. Without a solid understanding of the process of addition, the introduction of multiplication is frustrating and counterproductive. This principle also applies to Montessori activities and exercises outside of academics. Like mathematics, Practical Life manipulatives in the Casa are introduced in a specific order due to their sequential nature. Washing a Chalkboard, for instance, is almost always introduced before Washing a Table because there are fewer steps involved in Washing a Chalkboard. Also, a number of steps perfected during Washing a Chalkboard reappear during Washing a Table, making Washing a Chalkboard a foundational prerequisite. And yet, while almost no one questions the wisdom of introducing addition before multiplication, there is much concern about the fact that Montessori manipulatives outside of mathematics are subject to a similar form of sequential, structured learning. Naturally, there are exceptions when it comes to the order in which certain manipulatives are introduced. For example, while most children begin their Montessori education with Practical Life exercises,[19] some students may need to work with Sensorial, Language, or even Mathematics manipulatives first in order to best serve their individual physical, intellectual, and emotional needs.[20] Montessori education is respectful of the fact that every child is unique. One of the many incredible aspects of Montessori's child-centered philosophy is its ability to accommodate learning differences in order to help each student reach his fullest potential at his own pace.[21] This is obviously not the philosophy of an allegedly regimented educational system.

Although many Montessori manipulatives encourage a precise sequence of actions, there is room for creativity and independent discovery within the most structured tasks. Consider mathematics. It has already been established that the exactitude of mathematics leaves no room for opinion or dissent. This does not mean, however, that mathematics lacks a holistic, creative aspect. In the Montessori philosophy in particular, mathematics is not seen as a source of drudgery but a wondrous means of answering many of

---

[19] Montessori, Maria. *Creative Development in the Child*. Ed. Rukmini Ramachandran. Vol. 1. Chennai: Kalakshetra, 2007. Print. Pages 52-59, 95, 182-183.

[20] Montessori, Maria. *The Advanced Montessori Method I*. Vol. 9. Oxford: Clio, 2004. Print. The Clio Montessori Ser. Pages 67-75.

[21] Montessori, Maria. *Creative Development in the Child*. Ed. Rukmini Ramachandran. Vol. 1. Chennai: Kalakshetra, 2007. Print. Pages 206-207, 213-222.

life's problems and questions. Starting in the Primary prepared environment, students approximately four years of age and older learn how the precise nature of mathematics can be applied to a variety of interesting situations. A positive attitude toward mathematics begins with the open-ended nature of the Casa's scientifically designed, hands-on manipulatives. Rather than assigning boring workbook pages with rows of math problems to solve, the guide introduces activities such as "The Stamp Game" to help students create and solve their own original equations into the thousands using the four operations of mathematics: addition, subtraction, multiplication, and division. While bound by the laws of addition (2 + 2 will always equal 4), the child has the freedom to add any numbers of his choice together as long as the sum does not exceed 9,999, at least at first. As the child gains a greater understanding of the decimal system, he should eventually be able to manipulate numbers into the ten thousands, hundred thousands, and millions. "Word Problems" are presented to demonstrate the practical, real-world applications of the four operations of mathematics perfected in earlier exercises. Following practice, children are invited to create original Word Problems, which further fuels creativity. As students mature, they gain the ability to appreciate the wonder of mathematics on a grand scale, such as how mathematical calculations contribute to our understanding of the universe. Although the grandiose applications of mathematics are generally best suited to Montessori Elementary students, the origins of mathematical awareness begin in the Primary Casa. It is by learning the precise nature of mathematics, including the decimal system, that a future understanding of the universe and all its wonders becomes possible.[22]

Of course, mathematics is important, the skeptics may say, but we are talking about three through six year old children! Why

---

[22] Montessori, Maria. *To Educate the Human Potential*. Vol. 6. Oxford: Clio, 2003. Print. The Clio Montessori Ser. Pages 1-11.

should they concern themselves with such things? Why not just let them pursue completely creative tasks like art and music? This is certainly a legitimate concern considering that children under the age of six or seven were not expected to attend formal schooling until recent history. However, it is important to note that nothing in the Primary prepared environment is introduced in order to compete with international children who have the world's highest test scores. Everything that is introduced in the Casa is presented because it is age-appropriate and naturally appealing to three through six year old children. This includes complex subjects such as language and mathematics. For the sake of argument, let us set the matter of academics aside. What about creative activities such as art and music? Must these expressive exercises also follow an explicit sequence of actions? Absolutely! While there is certainly a great sense of freedom in art and music, these cultural extensions are also subject to natural limits based upon the confines of the materials used. Painting a picture, for example, is as orderly as washing a table or solving a mathematical equation. Before the creative process of painting a picture can begin, the child in the Casa must first gather all the necessary materials. The types of materials needed depend upon the medium that will be used. Watercolor brushes, for instance, may not be used for oil paints or damage will result. When the child has gathered his items and begins to paint, he is expected to keep his artistic creation on the piece of paper he has chosen. No one in a Montessori Primary prepared environment tells the child what he must paint, but the child is expected to gather the necessary materials, use the correct materials for each medium, hold brushes and use them correctly to prevent damage, keep the artwork on the paper, and clean up after himself when finished. The child has freedom of expression, as with any other Montessori manipulative, but that freedom is contained within natural limits which include following a logical, complete sequence of events from start to finish. The same is true of musical expression. When a child chooses to play a musical instrument following a presentation from the guide, he must use the instrument correctly. A drum is always struck with the mallet designed for that particular drum. The child may not use a xylophone mallet or a twig or a ruler to beat the drum as doing so constitutes improper use of the materials that can also cause permanent damage. Again, no one tells the child what tune to play, or that he must play a tune at all. All the child is compelled to do is use the material properly to prevent damage. When the student is introduced to music literacy manipulatives later in his Primary education, he also learns how to compose original music. As creative and beautiful as his musical compositions might be, he must still use correct music notation to transcribe his work so anyone in the future can enjoy it. True creativity and beauty can only come from a structured framework.[23]

What about the Sensorial area? Another common misconception about the Montessori Method is that certain manipulatives, such as the Pink Tower, may only be built one specific way without any deviation from the guide's official demonstration. While it is true that the guide typically begins by showing a child one specific way to perform a task, this practice is not meant to be dictatorial. Rather, by showing a child how to use a manipulative successfully in a single precise manner, the guide creates a solid starting point for the student's further independent exploration. Even within Montessori education, there are different schools of thought when it comes to presenting "variations," or giving additional lessons for a particular manipulative. One philosophy states that it is better for the guide to present the Pink Tower only one way so that the child can figure out a variety of other ways to build the Pink Tower by himself and experience the joy of discovery. The other philosophy states that the guide should demonstrate multiple ways to build the Pink Tower so the child

---

[23] Montessori, Maria. *The Advanced Montessori Method II*. Vol. 13. Oxford: Clio, 2006. Print. The Clio Montessori Ser. Pages 301-315, 319-379.

does not mistakenly believe that the guide only wants him to follow a prescribed activity sequence. Regardless of the particular philosophy a Montessorian follows, the basic principle of variations remains the same. Children are absolutely permitted, and encouraged, to make independent discoveries about the manipulatives presented in the Casa. There are, of course, natural limits when it comes to the child's explorations. The child may not use any material in a fashion that poses a danger to himself, others, or the material itself. He must also use the manipulative for its intended purpose. The Pink Tower, for example, is designed as an exploration of three dimensional change and should be used as such. It is not designed to be pushed around on the floor aimlessly without any purpose.[24] When a child moves manipulatives around without purpose, it could be a sign he is bored, frustrated,[25] or insufficiently challenged and needs assistance finding a more interesting and appropriate occupation that will also assist his holistic development.[26]

It is important to emphasize that the freedom afforded students in a Montessori Primary prepared environment is typically far greater than other forms of schooling. Traditional preschools and kindergartens, despite their fancy dollhouses, dress-up boxes, building blocks, and other forms of free play, are generally teacher-directed environments that adhere to a strict schedule. When the teacher decides it is story time, all the children must cease their activities to listen to a story, even if they have no interest. When it is snack time, all the children must eat snack at the same time, whether they are hungry or not. When it is recess, all the children must go outside when told, whether they want to play outside or not. When it is not recess, outdoor time is

---

[24] Montessori, Maria. *Creative Development in the Child.* Ed. Rukmini Ramachandran. Vol. 1. Chennai: Kalakshetra, 2007. Print. Pages 194-199.
[25] Montessori, Maria. *The Absorbent Mind.* Trans. Claude A. Claremont. Vol. 1. Oxford: Clio, 2004. Print. The Clio Montessori Ser. Pages 153-174, 180-182.
[26] Ibid.

forbidden, even if children want to work or play outside. These policies are in sharp contrast to how a child-centered Montessori Primary prepared environment is organized. When the guide tells a story, the children are invited, not forced, to gather and listen. When children are hungry, they prepare snacks on their own schedule. When children want to play outside, they enter the outdoor prepared environment at will as long as they are appropriately dressed for the weather. Yes, manipulatives are generally introduced and performed in a specific sequence. Yes, materials must be used with purpose and not shoved about aimlessly. Yes, there are natural limits for all activities, including art and music. But these rules are rational expectations based on the real world, not what the latest pop psychology and educational fads say children should be doing. In real life, actions are performed in logical sequences and natural consequences occur when tasks are performed incorrectly or in the wrong order. Within life's natural limits, there is great room for wonder, creativity, and discovery. And what better place is there to provide a foundation for a lifetime of wonder, creativity, and discovery than the Montessori Primary prepared environment?

References

Montessori, Maria. *The Absorbent Mind*. Trans. Claude A. Claremont. Vol. 1. Oxford: Clio, 2004. Print. The Clio Montessori Ser.

Montessori, Maria. *The Advanced Montessori Method I*. Vol. 9. Oxford: Clio, 2004. Print. The Clio Montessori Ser.

Montessori, Maria. *The Advanced Montessori Method II*. Vol. 13. Oxford: Clio, 2006. Print. The Clio Montessori Ser.

Montessori, Maria. *Creative Development in the Child*. Ed. Rukmini Ramachandran. Vol. 1. Chennai: Kalakshetra, 2007. Print.

Montessori, Maria. *Dr. Montessori's Own Handbook*. Mineola: Dover Publications, 2005. Print.

Montessori, Maria. *To Educate the Human Potential*. Vol. 6. Oxford: Clio, 2003. Print. The Clio Montessori Ser.

AN OVERVIEW OF MONTESSORI PRIMARY MATHEMATICS[27]

Introduction

Young children have a far greater capacity for mathematics than mainstream education gives them credit for. According to the Common Core State Standards Initiative, a kindergarten student should be able to count to 100, read and write the numerals from 0 through 20, and add and subtract within the number ten.[28] While this standard may seem advanced for a five or six year old, it is not as comprehensive as the extensive mathematics curriculum presented in an authentic Montessori Primary program for two-and-a-half through six year old students. In a Montessori Casa, or Primary prepared environment, students approximately four years of age and older routinely perform addition, subtraction, multiplication, and division problems into the thousands using hands-on manipulatives. Around five-and-a-half or six years of age, numbers and mathematical operations into the millions, including story problems, are introduced. How is this possible with children so young? To answer this question, it helps to understand the foundation a child receives in the Casa in order to enthusiastically apply himself to mathematics while simultaneously exhibiting comprehension of such a complex subject.

---

[27] This article features edited excerpts from *Montessori Primary Addition* by Mary Da Prato, © 2017.

[28] "Kindergarten » Counting & Cardinality." *Common Core State Standards Initiative: Preparing America's Students for College and Career*. Common Core State Standards Initiative, 2018. Web. 18 Apr. 2018. <http://www.corestandards.org/Math/Content/K/CC/>.

An Overview of Montessori's Mathematics Philosophy and Practice

In the Casa, or Montessori classroom for two-and-a-half through six year old students, mathematics is introduced in a hands-on, age-appropriate manner in alignment with young children's natural interests and tendencies. As a complex subject that requires many holistic prerequisite skills for optimal results, mathematics is introduced only when a child demonstrates cognitive readiness. Readiness for official mathematics lessons usually does not present itself before four years of age, although an individual student may be ready for his first mathematics presentation earlier or later than the recommended age. Due to the intellectual nature of mathematics, it is better not to rush a child into abstract ideas even if he has attained the suggested age for the initial Number Rods presentation.[29] Mathematics may only be introduced once a child has a solid foundation in all essential prerequisite skills, even if this means he will begin studying mathematics at a later date than his peers.

It is vital to remember that Montessori is not a competitive method of education designed to make children learn concepts as quickly and as early as possible. Instead, Montessori Primary education is designed to present hands-on, developmentally appropriate experiences in alignment with the universal needs and interests of two-and-a-half through six year old children when the time is appropriate for each individual child. The trained Montessori guide knows the optimal time to present lessons to each child in her class based upon her training, experience, and keen observations of individual students' progress. Each child is unique and learns at his own pace. The Montessori guide respects the child's individual cognitive development and presents lessons

---

[29] Da Prato, Mary. *My First Montessori Book of Quantities.* Seattle: CreateSpace Independent Publishing Platform, 2014.

according to the student's readiness rather than during an arbitrarily imposed timeline created by adults.

In accordance with the philosophy of child-centered education, Montessori Primary guides generally do not concern themselves with testing or data regarding local, national, and international test scores in mathematics. Through hands-on, cognitively appropriate presentations, children become immersed in a math-positive atmosphere uninhibited by the unnatural pressure of mainstream expectations. Without having to worry about test scores and how well they compare to their peers, Montessori students are at liberty to explore the wonder of mathematics unhampered by artificially imposed, external pressure. This humane, individualized, holistic approach to mathematics presented at the child's own pace fosters friendliness toward error coupled with an innate desire for accuracy. In the Casa, children are not afraid to make mathematical errors because there are no punitive red marks given on a paper for incorrect answers. Instead, children learn from the materials themselves through the self-correcting nature of the manipulatives known as "control of error."[30] Unlike an embarrassing bad grade, control of error helps the child correct his own mistakes, which cultivates a desire to achieve accuracy. The attainment of accuracy, especially in mathematics in which there is typically only one correct answer, is an attractive accomplishment to a young learner. Conquering a math problem aided by the Casa's friendly, self-directed environment provides a solid foundation for a lifelong love of mathematics as its own reward.

How Mathematics Is Defined in the Casa

Mathematics is the abstract science of quantity, number, and space. "Quantity" refers to the amount of a given item in a defined

---

[30] Montessori, Maria. *The Absorbent Mind.* Trans. Claude A. Claremont. Vol. 1. Oxford: Clio, 2004. Print. The Clio Montessori Ser. Pages 223-229.

context such as *one* pencil, *two* blocks, or *three* beads. "Number" refers to the specific numerical symbols used to accurately describe quantities in writing such as *1* pencil, *2* blocks, or *3* beads. In the wider world, the terms "quantity" and "number" are often used interchangeably. To provide clarity in mathematics for young children, "quantity" and "number" are presented as distinct, albeit related, ideas in the Casa. "Space," the third aspect of mathematics, describes the structure of a given environment such as the maximum capacity of a classroom or gymnasium. Students in the Montessori Casa explore all three aspects of mathematics through interactive individual and small group activities that encourage independent learning and discovery following an initial presentation from the trained Montessori teacher, or guide.

How Mathematics Is Introduced in the Casa

In the Primary prepared environment, mathematics is introduced in a hands-on, concrete, sensorial manner best suited to the natural learning patterns of young children. Starting at approximately four years of age, children are formally introduced to official, hands-on mathematics materials that provide the foundation for all future mathematics studies in the Montessori curriculum. The first official mathematics presentation in the Casa is "Number Rods," a manipulative consisting of ten wooden bars with alternating red and blue painted sections. These precisely measured Number Rods, which range from ten centimeters to one hundred centimeters (one meter) in length, give students their first sensorial impression of quantities as isolated entities through the senses of sight and touch.

Prerequisites for Mathematical Success

Although children under four years of age are typically not cognitively ready for official mathematics presentations, preparations for joyful mathematic success begin on the first day of school when the child is two-and-a-half or three years of age. Popular children's songs that include counting such as "Ten Little Horses" and "Five Green and Speckled Frogs" are introduced to small groups of three to seven children as early as possible to promote music appreciation and mathematical awareness. In addition to singing, young students may also be exposed to numbers and counting during "transition times" in the Casa. Transition times or transition periods occur before the uninterrupted three hour morning work period, before lunch, after lunch when the young students typically prepare to go home for the afternoon, and after the uninterrupted afternoon work period when it is time for older students to go home. To help facilitate a smooth transfer from one transition period to the next, the guide or her assistant may entertain the children with simple number and counting games that can be played while students are waiting in line to use the sink before lunch or waiting during pick-up time at the end of the day. For example, while waiting for parents to arrive during pick-up time, the assistant may help keep the waiting students engaged by saying, "Let's see how many seconds it takes for the next parent to arrive!" The aide and students then count together starting with the number "one" until the next parent arrives. When the parent arrives, counting begins again from the number "one" while waiting for the next parent's arrival. This game can also be adapted for other long waiting periods such as when children are waiting in line to use the sink before lunch. Besides keeping antsy children busy, this counting exercise exposes young students to the sequence of numbers and subtly instills an awareness of the passage of time in seconds. To provide variety during transition times, the guide or aide may also initiate "The Zero Game." Similar to "Simon Says," The Zero Game gives individual students simple commands with the added bonus of incorporating numbers through nine. To play The Zero Game, the guide or aide says something like, "Clap your hands seven times, (Name)." Once the child completes the task, the adult chooses another child to perform a numbered command. For children under four or those with little counting experience, the adult gives a command using a "one" or a "two" as most students can count that high. At some point in the game, the guide or aide introduces a "zero" command such as, "Tap your toes zero times, (Name)." Like Simon Says, this part of the game exercises the child's understanding and ability to do nothing when given a command involving zero. Due to the abstract nature of "zero," these commands are reserved for children who have prior experience with the number zero through the "Spindle Boxes," a mathematics activity in which students bundle specific quantities of spindles together and place them in their corresponding numbered compartments. Even though young students playing The Zero Game are often limited to commands of "one" or "two" due to their limited counting experience, they are exposed to the numbers "zero" through "nine" by participating in this non-competitive exercise for children ages two-and-a-half through six. Select classical nursery rhymes and songs with counting such as "One, Two, Buckle my Shoe," "Hickory Dickory Dock," and "This Old Man," may also be recited or sung for both entertainment and counting practice during long waiting periods. These rhymes may also be performed during small group presentations during the uninterrupted three hour work period.

In addition to singing and transition activities, young children in the Casa are also exposed to counting and numbers through observation of older peers at work. In the Primary prepared environment, there is no pre-determined "mathematics time" in which all students must cease their activities in order to complete mathematics assignments. Instead, students in the Casa are provided with an uninterrupted three hour work period in which they may choose any available individual or small group activity as long as they have had an initial presentation from the guide. At any given moment during the work period, there will be children of different ages and skill levels working with materials from a variety of subject areas. Freedom of movement, an essential feature of any high-functioning Montessori Casa, allows students to unobtrusively observe their peers. By observing classmates, children may learn skills or obtain insights that would not have been possible if observation were prevented.[31] Observation also allows young students to see higher level mathematics exercises in use by their older, more experienced classmates which provides a glimpse of the exciting new activities that await them in the future. When a child observes other children in his classroom community happily and voluntarily working with mathematics activities, he subconsciously absorbs the Casa's math-positive atmosphere which helps prevent future anxiety about the subject.[32]

Besides observing peers at work, young students who have not yet had a lesson in the observed activity are allowed to dust materials of interest as a purposeful means of exploration in anticipation of future lessons. The guide may also modify official mathematics presentations to satisfy curious young students at a more cognitively appropriate level. For instance, if a young student is attracted to the beautiful glass color-coded beads in the "Addition Snake Game," the guide may select a handful of beads from the activity for the child to sort into groups by color. By allowing the child to perform cognitively appropriate tasks with the mathematics materials, even though the student is not yet ready for an official presentation, the guide supports visual, tactile, and baric exploration of the Casa's manipulatives in preparation for future studies.

---

[31] Montessori, Maria. *The Absorbent Mind.* Trans. Claude A. Claremont. Vol. 1. Oxford: Clio, 2004. Print. The Clio Montessori Ser. Pages 205-208.
[32] Montessori, Maria. *Creative Development in the Child.* Ed. Rukmini Ramachandran. Vol. 1. Chennai: Kalakshetra, 2007. Print. Pages 132-134.

The Memory Game of Numbers

Dusting and sorting beads are not the only means of purposeful mathematics exploration for young children in the Casa. With some assistance, young students who are interested can also participate in "The Memory Game of Numbers" alongside their older, more mathematically experienced peers. The Memory Game of Numbers, an activity designed to test a student's understanding of the numbers zero through ten, is an enjoyable way for students approximately four years of age and older to apply their newfound counting skills. During The Memory Game of Numbers, each child in the group draws a slip of paper from a dish, bag, or basket. Each slip of paper has one number written on it from "0" to "10." When it is the child's turn, he must remember his number and retrieve a corresponding quantity of objects from the room. A child who draws the number "8," for example, must bring eight like objects to the group such as eight buttons or eight cotton balls. While seemingly simple, the ability to accurately retrieve physical quantities based upon an unspoken numerical symbol requires a solid understanding of the numbers "0" through "10," a level of knowledge that is typically not achieved until a child is at least four years of age and has mastered all essential prerequisite skills. Despite The Memory Game of Numbers' advanced gameplay, a child under four years of age in the Casa can still participate with the help of a willing, older peer. If interested, a young child may ask an older, mathematically experienced friend to help him play The Memory Game of Numbers. When this occurs, the older child plays The Memory Game of Numbers as usual, albeit with a younger peer in tow while he retrieves the quantity of items indicated by the number on his slip. Depending upon the age and cognitive level of the younger child, he may simply follow the older child around while he plays the game. A slightly older child who is nearly ready for an official presentation may be more involved in the retrieval of objects.[33] Every child is unique. The guide observes any spontaneous student interest in mathematics and notes observations in her records.

Practical Life Preparation for Mathematics

Early exposure to mathematics through counting games, songs, nursery rhymes, observation of older peers, dusting materials of interest, sorting mathematics materials by color, and participating in The Memory Game of Numbers alongside older peers are only a small fraction of the experiences that pave the way for successful work with mathematics. The most important preparation for mathematics, which also begins on the first day of school, is work with "Practical Life" activities. Practical Life, one of four main subject areas in the Casa, focuses on activities that help children practice and acquire gross and fine motor development while learning culturally relevant practical life skills. The skills developed in Practical Life are categorized into five equally important, parallel categories:[34] Social Relations, Control and Coordination of Movement, Preliminary Activities, Care of the Person, and Care of the Environment. "Social Relations" or "Grace and Courtesy" comprises activities which model and reinforce manners, common classroom procedures, and peaceful conflict resolution skills. "Control and Coordination of Movement" focuses upon development of gross motor control through fun, age-appropriate activities such as "Walking on the Line," an ellipse marked on the floor where children can practice rhythm and balance. "Preliminary Activities," such as "Opening and Closing Containers" and "Folding,"[35] allow children to practice fine motor

---

[33] Montessori, Maria. *The Absorbent Mind.* Trans. Claude A. Claremont. Vol. 1. Oxford: Clio, 2004. Print. The Clio Montessori Ser. Pages 206-207.

[34] "Expression" or "Expression Exercises" such as art and music are also classified as Practical Life activities in AMI classrooms. In other Montessori traditions, art, music, and similar disciplines may be called "Cultural Extensions."

control in isolation from more complex exercises in preparation for future Practical Life work. "Care of the Person" activities such as "Dressing Frames" to fasten and unfasten common clothing closures and "Hand Washing" give children the tools they need to learn, practice, and perfect skills related to hygiene and functional independence. "Care of the Environment" exercises such as "Washing a Table" and "Washing the Leaves of a Plant" show students how to care for their classroom environment, indoor plants, and pets to foster environmental responsibility for both living things and inanimate objects. Collectively, these five categories of Practical Life provide the basis for all future work in the Casa, including academic success.[36] Beyond introducing and reinforcing manners, gross and fine motor coordination, hygiene, personal responsibility, environmental responsibility, and functional independence, the naturally appealing Practical Life exercises also foster spontaneous concentration. Concentration upon freely chosen Practical Life activities[37] during the Casa's uninterrupted three hour work period provides the essential foundation for a phenomenon known as "normalization."[38] Normalization is the process in which a young child spontaneously abandons all negative behaviors in exchange for positive behaviors.[39] The behaviors of a normalized child include kindness, patience, helpfulness, empathy, [40] hospitality,[41] pride in one's

---

[35] "Folding" is a presentation in the Casa in which a student folds cloth squares into squares, triangles, rectangles, and thirds in preparation for practical folding work such as folding towels, napkins, letters for envelopes, and origami.

[36] Montessori, Maria. *Creative Development in the Child*. Ed. Rukmini Ramachandran. Vol. 1. Chennai: Kalakshetra, 2007. Print. Pages 175-183, 192-199, 206-207, 212.

[37] Ibid. Pages 182-183.

[38] Montessori, Maria. *The Absorbent Mind*. Trans. Claude A. Claremont. Vol. 1. Oxford: Clio, 2004. Print. The Clio Montessori Ser. Pages 182-188, 190-191, 202, 204.

[39] Ibid. Pages 183-188, 190.

[40] Ibid. Pages 183-188.

individual accomplishments, joy for the success of others,[42] inner discipline,[43] self-regulation, self-confidence,[44] voluntary rejection of external rewards,[45] and the ability to choose activities and concentrate upon them without adult interference or guidance.[46] It is only after an individual student is normalized that enthusiastic academic achievement becomes possible. [47] [48] In conjunction with the acquisition of normalization, Practical Life exercises prepare students for mathematics by cultivating holistic skills essential for joyful academic success. The traits acquired in Practical Life that provide a vital foundation for mathematical success include self-control, well-developed gross and fine motor coordination, spontaneous concentration, the ability to follow a logical sequence of actions from memory, patience, precision, exactness, perseverance, and accuracy. These qualities are developed naturally at the child's own pace through hands-on work with increasingly advanced Practical Life exercises.

Dressing Frames as Preparation for Mathematics

A new two-and-a-half or three year old student may begin his Practical Life education with a "Dressing Frame," an activity designed to help children practice and master closures relevant to

---

[41] Montessori, Maria. *The Secret of Childhood.* Trans. Barbara B. Carter. Hyderabad: Orient Longman, 2006. Print. Pages 133-135, 137.

[42] Montessori, Maria. *The Absorbent Mind.* Trans. Claude A. Claremont. Vol. 1. Oxford: Clio, 2004. Print. The Clio Montessori Ser. Pages 210-211, 220.

[43] Ibid. Pages 183-184.

[44] Montessori, Maria. *The Secret of Childhood.* Trans. Barbara B. Carter. Hyderabad: Orient Longman, 2006. Print. Pages 177-178.

[45] Ibid. Pages 128-129.

[46] Ibid. Pages 92-94.

[47] Montessori, Maria. *Dr. Montessori's Own Handbook.* Mineola: Dover Publications, 2005. Print. Pages 91-94, 117.

[48] Montessori, Maria. *The Child, Society, and the World: Unpublished Speeches and Writings.* Vol. 7. Oxford: Clio, 2006. Print. The Clio Montessori Ser. Pages 21-22.

the culture such as buttons, zippers, and Velcro.™ The first Dressing Frame typically presented to a child in the Casa is the "Snap Frame." Although seemingly irrelevant to mathematics, fastening and unfastening Dressing Frame snaps from top to bottom instills the internal and external qualities necessary for academic success. For instance, each Dressing Frame requires a logical sequence of actions. To use the Snap Frame, the child must open the snaps before he can close them. The act of fastening and unfastening snaps on the Snap Frame, working from top to bottom, is a simple two-step sequence of repeated actions. As the child advances to more difficult Dressing Frames, such as the Buckle Frame and the Bow Tying Frame, the sequence of actions becomes increasingly complex. The ability to follow a prescribed sequence of actions is essential for solving mathematics problems in the future. Like fastening and unfastening various Dressing Frames, each mathematical equation has a specific sequence of actions that must be performed in order to achieve the desired result.

In addition to learning and applying complex sequences of actions from memory, children who use the Dressing Frames also practice and perfect their fine motor control. Children need to perfect their manual dexterity in order to successfully use the Casa's hands-on mathematics manipulatives in the future. Many mathematics manipulatives require students to carefully handle and count small glass beads that represent quantities. The ability to safely transport and accurately count the Casa's bead materials requires inner-discipline and perfected fine motor control, traits developed by working extensively with Practical Life materials including the Dressing Frames. Due to the Casa's uninterrupted three hour work period, children also have the opportunity to cultivate patience, perseverance, and exactitude through Practical Life exercises without artificial interruptions to their work in the form of arbitrary class assignments or blaring school bells.

In the child-centered environment of the Casa, students have ample time to learn and perfect the skills necessary for future academic achievement.

Sewing a Button as a Preparation for Mathematics

Another Practical Life preparation for mathematics may include "Sewing a Button." An advanced Practical Life activity for children roughly four to four-and-a-half years of age, Sewing a Button requires patience, precision, exactness, attention to detail, perseverance, and accuracy. These traits, developed early in the child's education through sequentially organized Practical Life exercises, prepare children for joyful, successful work with mathematics. The child's patience and precision when threading a needle is akin to the patience and precision required when laying out the Casa's mathematics materials. Once the needle is threaded, the ability to push it in and out of the button holes in an exact sequence calls upon the child's will to work carefully and accurately in order to secure the button to the cloth swatch. Mathematics requires the same care and attention to detail in order to achieve the desired outcome. When the button is sewn securely onto the cloth, the child verifies his work by pulling gently on the button. If the button does not come loose, he has done the task correctly. If the button comes undone, the child works to root out his error in order to achieve the desired result. No one has to tell the child he sewed the button incorrectly as the material itself provides the necessary feedback. This self-correcting device present in many Montessori materials is called "control of error."[49]

---

[49] In the Casa, "control of error" usually pertains to Sensorial and Mathematics materials. The Practical Life equivalent is the "point of interest," which may have to be modeled by the guide rather than demonstrated through the material itself. In the case of an improperly secured button becoming loose, it may be unnecessary for the guide to give a verbal or modeled point of interest as the detachment of the button signifies a clear control of error.

When a child corrects his own mistakes with the assistance of control of error, he develops friendliness toward error coupled with a desire to attain accuracy.[50] Like the button sewn onto a cloth swatch, mathematics also requires a degree of verification and friendliness toward error. If a problem is solved incorrectly, there are measures built into the Montessori mathematics manipulatives to help students discover and correct their own mistakes without the embarrassment of a teacher telling them they did something "wrong" either orally or on paper in the form of red marks on a test or a bad grade. Early, extensive experience with an array of increasingly advanced Practical Life exercises, including "Sewing a Button," make rewards and punishments unnecessary for learning.[51] Collectively, Practical Life activities foster concentration, normalization, and the acquisition of internal qualities essential for future academic success and a lifelong love of learning in all areas including mathematics.[52]

Sensorial Preparation for Mathematics

In addition to Practical Life exercises, children in the Casa are also prepared for mathematics through precisely measured, scientifically designed "Sensorial" materials. Sensorial manipulatives allow students to focus upon the five senses of vision, hearing, touch, smell, and taste as well as their qualities. "Qualities" are the specific aspects of a given sense. The sense of vision, for example, has three qualities or aspects that can be perceived by the human eye: dimension, color, and shape. Each Sensorial quality is explored in a separate Montessori

---

[50] Montessori, Maria. *The Absorbent Mind*. Trans. Claude A. Claremont. Vol. 1. Oxford: Clio, 2004. Print. The Clio Montessori Ser. Pages 223-229.
[51] Ibid. Pages 182-188, 190-191, 202, 204, 224.
[52] Montessori, Maria. *Creative Development in the Child*. Ed. Rukmini Ramachandran. Vol. 1. Chennai: Kalakshetra, 2007. Print. Pages 132-134, 175-183, 192-199, 206-207, 212.

manipulative. "Mixed Impressions" manipulatives, which combine two or more sensorial qualities, are introduced following experience with each quality in isolation.

One of the earliest Sensorial presentations a young child in the Casa receives is the "Cylinder Blocks," a series of manipulatives that explore the visual quality of dimension. By taking precisely measured cylinders in and out of their corresponding holes in a Cylinder Block, a two-and-a-half to three year old child develops an understanding of spatial relationships and practices 1:1 correspondence. "1:1 correspondence," the simplest form of mathematics, is the ability to match an object to its corresponding item. A practical illustration of 1:1 correspondence is place settings at a dinner table. Children as young as two may discover that each member of the family receives one plate, one cup, and one set of silverware. In this example, one set of tableware corresponds to one person. The Casa's four Cylinder Blocks concretely demonstrate and reinforce 1:1 correspondence in preparation for future work in mathematics.

In addition to Cylinder Blocks, 1:1 correspondence is also introduced and reinforced through all Sensorial materials that involve "pairing" or matching an item to its corresponding material. This important mathematical process is not limited to Sensorial materials for the visual sense. 1:1 correspondence can also be explored by matching grain-filled "Sound Cylinders" by auditory volume and "Movable Bells" by pitch. Graded sandpaper "Touch Tablets" and "Fabric Boxes" containing fabric swatches of various textures foster 1:1 correspondence with the sense of touch. "Smelling Jars" permit 1:1 correspondence through the olfactory sense. "Tasting Bottles" allow 1:1 correspondence of bitter, sour, salty, and sweet liquids by taste. These are only a sampling of the Sensorial materials in the Casa that encourage 1:1 correspondence in preparation for sensorial awareness as a prerequisite to mathematics. There are more than a dozen Sensorial pairing exercises in the Casa that foster 1:1 correspondence as a concrete foundation for mathematics.

Sensorial Grading Activities

Activities that involve pairing to strengthen 1:1 correspondence are only the beginning of a child's Sensorial education in the Casa. Following success with pairing a given Sensorial manipulative, it is often possible to introduce "grading." Grading is the ability to arrange materials in a logical sequence, a more difficult task than matching like items. When a student grades Sensorial manipulatives, such as arranging Color Tablets from light to dark or dark to light, he concretely explores the relationships between and among Sensorial qualities. The ability to compare and examine Sensorial relationships is an essential prerequisite for mathematical success.[53]

Sensorial Three Period Lessons

In addition to pairing and grading, Sensorial activities in the Casa promote vocabulary acquisition as well as strengthen long and short-term memory. Following hands-on experience with a given Sensorial manipulative, children learn the names of the materials. In the Casa, experience almost always precedes language. It is essential that students have ample hands-on experience with manipulatives before learning their accompanying vocabulary due to young children's sensorial acquisition of learning. Learning the word "rhombus," for example, has no meaning for a young child without having actually seen, touched, and traced a concrete, physical representation of a rhombus.[54] Once a child has experienced a rhombus as well as other geometric shapes at a purely sensorial level, the guide introduces contrasting

---

[53] Montessori, Maria. *Dr. Montessori's Own Handbook.* Mineola: Dover Publications, 2005. Print. Pages 116-129.
[54] Ibid. Pages 18, 50-64, 79-87, 93-95.

shape names three at a time in the form of a "Three Period Lesson." The Three Period Lesson, a naturally appealing, game-like technique used to introduce vocabulary in the Casa, is used with materials and names from all subject areas including mathematics. Long before receiving an official mathematics presentation, children are familiarized with the Three Period Lesson through vocabulary lessons pertaining to Practical Life and Sensorial activities. An example of an early Three Period Lesson with previously introduced Sensorial materials is learning the names of the shapes. While many students are able to identify circles, squares, and triangles upon entering the Casa, the Montessori Primary curriculum enhances and expands children's early experiences with shapes by introducing the forms and names of many polygons as well as the seven types of triangles. No vocabulary is too difficult for a child under six or seven years of age due to his instinctual attraction to language.[55] In addition to indirectly preparing students for future geometry studies, shape identification is also an important preparation for literacy as letters and numbers are also represented by specific shapes.[56]

To initiate a Three Period Lesson with shape names, the guide invites an individual student who has been working with the Geometry Cabinet to play a game with her. After the child accepts the invitation, the guide chooses three shapes from the Geometry Cabinet with contrasting forms and names, such as the rectangle, the hexagon, and the equilateral triangle. The guide places her three chosen shapes on a tray and carries them to a table or rug. Once the tray is placed on the workspace, the guide chooses one of the three shapes and isolates it in front of the child. She points to the isolated shape and identifies it by saying, "This is the

---

[55] Montessori, Maria. *The Absorbent Mind*. Trans. Claude A. Claremont. Vol. 1. Oxford: Clio, 2004. Print. The Clio Montessori Ser. Pages 159-162.

[56] Montessori, Maria. *Creative Development in the Child*. Ed. Rukmini Ramachandran. Vol. 1. Chennai: Kalakshetra, 2007. Print. Pages 123-127, 138-145.

rectangle." After naming the first shape, the guide removes a second shape from the tray and places it in front of the child beside the first shape with some space left between the two shapes. Pointing to the second shape, she says, "This is the hexagon." The guide then selects the final shape from the tray, isolates it in front of the child, and says, "This is the equilateral triangle." To review the introduced vocabulary, the guide points to each of the three shapes in turn and says, "This is the rectangle. This is the hexagon. This is the equilateral triangle." This concludes "Naming," the first period of the Three Period Lesson.

After naming each of the three shapes, the guide begins the second period of the Three Period Lesson, known as "Recognition." During Recognition, the guide gives commands with the three shapes to reinforce the newly introduced vocabulary. Examples of commands include, "Trace the equilateral triangle," "Move the rectangle here," or "Point to the hexagon." After giving a few commands, the guide may have the child close his eyes while she mixes up the shapes to make the game more challenging. Once the guide is finished rearranging the shapes, she tells the child to open his eyes. The game continues with additional commands as before. If the child hesitates or gives an incorrect answer at any time during Recognition, the guide states the correct answer without commentary or criticism as in, "This is the hexagon. Now show me the equilateral triangle." The second period of the Three Period Lesson continues until the child is confident with the vocabulary or loses interest.

The Third Period of the Three Period Lesson is called "Remembering." During this final stage of the Three Period Lesson, the guide points to a random shape and asks the child, "What is this?" She points to the other two shapes in turn and asks the same question. As always, if the child gives an incorrect answer, the guide states the correct answer without commentary or criticism. Once the child correctly identifies each of the three shapes, the guide asks if he would like to learn three more. If the child is interested, the guide puts away the shapes and chooses three new contrasting shapes. She then repeats the Three Period Lesson with the new shapes. If the child is uninterested in learning additional shape vocabulary at the moment, the guide and child put the shapes away for another day. Regardless of interest level, typically no more than six vocabulary words per category are introduced per day to prevent overwhelming the child.

Following several Three Period Lessons and reviews over the course of a few days, the guide introduces "Extensions of the Second Period," also known as "Bring Me Games," as well as "Extensions of the Third Period" to refine the child's long-term memory of recently introduced vocabulary. During the Extension of the Second Period or Bring Me Game for shape names, the guide lays out a few familiar shapes on a table or rug. She then sits on a chair or stool at a distance from the shapes. Depending upon the child's level of confidence with the shape vocabulary, the guide may sit a few feet away from the shapes or sit at the other end of the room. Once seated at the appropriate distance, the guide gives the child a "Bring Me" command such as "Bring me the hexagon." The child must then remember the guide's verbal instructions while he walks over to the table or rug containing the shapes, choose the correct shape, and bring the shape to the guide. If the child retrieves the correct shape, the guide affirms his accuracy by saying, "You brought me the hexagon. You can take the hexagon back."[57] After the child returns the hexagon to the workspace, he returns to the guide to receive additional "Bring Me" commands. If the child retrieves an incorrect shape at any time during the game, the guide affirms his choice by saying

---

[57] A Montessori guide is careful to choose words which foster independent student learning. To promote joyful, spontaneous learning, the guide tells the child he "can" take the hexagon back rather than he "may" take the hexagon back. The word "can" affirms the child's newfound abilities whereas "may" implies that the child must seek the guide's permission to perform a task he is ready to undertake.

something like, "Oh! You brought me the equilateral triangle. Now bring me the hexagon." The game continues until all the shapes are retrieved or until interest wanes. To end the game, the guide says, "Thank you for playing with me. What would you like to do now?" Following cleanup, life in the Casa continues as usual. The guide notes the lesson in her records before resuming her other duties.

A child who has played several Bring Me Games with many shapes over a period of time may be invited to play "Extensions of the Third Period." In this individual or small group activity, the guide invites the experienced child or a group of experienced children to play a game with her. Once gathered at a rug, the guide says, "Let's name all of the geometric shapes we can think of… like squares!" Students then participate in the majority of the activity, calling out shapes one at a time as they think of them. If there is a lull in the game, the guide may say, "Let's think of some more geometric shapes like right-angled scalene triangles!" The game continues until the children lose interest or cannot think of any more shapes. To conclude the activity, the guide thanks the child or children for playing with her and then dismisses her students one at a time. Following dismissal, the guide notes the activity in her records before resuming other work. Older, literate children who are confident with the presented vocabulary may further practice and solidify their knowledge by labelling shapes with typed or hand-written labels. The guide presents this written language extension when she observes interest and readiness.

Besides strengthening memory, Second and Third Period Extensions of the initial Three Period Lesson help the child build mental abstractions of sensorial qualities solely in his mind. Extension activities with shapes, for example, help the child mentally construct an abstraction, or permanent mental image, of different shapes in the absence of visual aids. When a child creates an abstraction of a hexagon, he will no longer need to look at or touch a physical hexagon to understand what the word "hexagon" means.[58] Hands-on practice with extension activities solidifies the concept of a hexagon for future use. The process of creating mental abstractions through hands-on experience becomes especially important when the student begins formal mathematics studies as mathematical concepts build heavily upon memory and prior learning. Creating the mental building blocks for short-term memory, long-term memory, and solid comprehension of sensorial qualities begins with the Sensorial manipulatives.[59] By working with the Casa's scientifically designed, hands-on Sensorial activities, children are able to mentally catalogue sensorial abstractions that provide the basis for mathematical understanding in the future.[60]

Review of Preparations for Mathematics

As evidenced by the previous Practical Life, Sensorial, and activity suggestions, hands-on, age-appropriate, concrete preparation for mathematics in the Casa is extensive and time consuming. Mathematics is not a subject that should be artificially pushed, forced, or rushed. Instead, readiness for mathematics begins with the child-centered, holistic foundation provided by the scientifically designed manipulatives and activities presented at the appropriate time within the Casa's uninterrupted three hour work period.[61] Although many of these exercises, particularly those in the Sensorial area, may be better reserved for classroom use,[62] you can support mathematics awareness and readiness at home starting

---

[58] Montessori, Maria. *Creative Development in the Child*. Ed. Rukmini Ramachandran. Vol. 1. Chennai: Kalakshetra, 2007. Print. Pages 108-114.

[59] Montessori, Maria. *The Discovery of the Child*. Trans. Mary A. Johnstone. Madras: Kalakshetra, 2006. Print. Pages 184-205, 208-209.

[60] Montessori, Maria. *Dr. Montessori's Own Handbook*. Mineola: Dover Publications, 2005. Print. Pages 116-129.

[61] Ibid. Pages 94, 116-129.

[62] Montessori, Maria. *The Discovery of the Child*. Trans. Mary A. Johnstone. Madras: Kalakshetra, 2006. Print. Pages 139-144.

when your child is two-and-a-half to three years of age in the following ways:

• Casually introduce and reinforce counting with your child when you perform daily tasks. When shopping at the store, count the number of apples or cans of soup aloud as you place them into your shopping cart or bag. Encourage your child to count with you by saying, "I need to buy *three* apples. Let's count them together!" As you put each apple in your cart or bag, count aloud, "One, two, three. I have *three* apples." Keep your counting excursions fun and upbeat. Do not worry at this point if your child actually understands what "three" means, even after consistent modeling. Children in the Casa, normalized or not, typically lack a solid understanding of quantities and their corresponding numerical symbols until they begin to receive official presentations with the Number Rods around four years of age.[63] [64]

• Sing fun songs and recite nursery rhymes related to counting with your child. Examples of popular counting songs and rhymes for children include, "This Old Man," "Hickory Dickory Dock," "Ten Little Horses," "Five Green and Speckled Frogs," and "One, Two, Buckle My Shoe." The lyrics to these songs and rhymes are available online. To introduce a song, sit at a rug with your child and say, "Let's sing a song!" Start singing without further commentary. Allow your child to join in when ready. If the song is short, say, "Let's sing it again!" After a couple

---

[63] Montessori, Maria. *Dr. Montessori's Own Handbook*. Mineola: Dover Publications, 2005. Print. Pages 117-122, 128-129.

[64] Montessori, Maria. *The California Lectures of Maria Montessori, 1915: Collected Speeches and Writings*. Ed. Robert G. Buckenmeyer. Vol. 15. Oxford: Clio, 2000. Print. The Clio Montessori Ser. Pages 77, 81.

of repetitions, say, "Thank you for singing with me." Ask your child what he would like to do next or simply transition to the next activity. Repeat the song daily over the next few days or when your child is interested. Keep in mind that some children like to sing along shortly after learning a new song while others would rather listen. A child who chooses to listen silently rather than actively participate internalizes the song[65] and may participate later. Music is important for young minds, whether or not your child is an active and enthusiastic participant.[66] Respect your child's choice whether to participate in a song or not. Observe his level of interest at all times.

• Always be positive about mathematics in front of your child. If you convey distaste or fear of the subject, your child may subconsciously absorb your anxieties about mathematics and numbers.[67] [68] Show friendliness toward error coupled with a desire to attain accuracy if you make a mathematics error. You can convey this positive attitude toward mathematics by cheerfully saying, "Oh! I forgot to carry the one. I have to go back and fix that." Even if your child does not understand what it means to "carry the one" or what you are doing, your cheerful voice and attitude toward addition and mathematics in general provide good modeling for your child's future academic achievement.[69]

---

[65] Montessori, Maria. *Creative Development in the Child.* Ed. Rukmini Ramachandran. Vol. 1. Chennai: Kalakshetra, 2007. Print. Pages 222-236.
[66] Montessori, Maria. *The Discovery of the Child.* Trans. Mary A. Johnstone. Madras: Kalakshetra, 2006. Print. Pages 319-325.
[67] Montessori, Maria. *Creative Development in the Child.* Ed. Rukmini Ramachandran. Vol. 1. Chennai: Kalakshetra, 2007. Print. Pages 133-134.
[68] Montessori, Maria. *What You Should Know about Your Child.* Vol. 4. Amsterdam: Montessori-Pierson, 2008. Print.
The Montessori Ser. Page 61-66.
[69] Montessori, Maria. *The Absorbent Mind.* Trans. Claude A. Claremont. Vol. 1.

• Offer relevant, culturally appropriate, appealing Practical Life exercises in your home that promote spontaneous concentration as an essential foundation for normalization.[70] Normalization is the process in which a young child abandons all negative behaviors in exchange for positive behaviors.[71] The traits acquired through normalization allow joyful, academic achievement, including mathematics, to naturally occur.[72] [73] As an internal quality, normalization cannot be externally imposed or forced. Instead, the adult must create a prepared environment conducive to the acquisition of normalization.[74] If possible, begin by placing your child's activities on open shelving to encourage a sense of order and aesthetics instead of throwing articles into a disorganized toy chest.

• Involve your child under careful adult supervision with daily household tasks such as measuring pet food, watering indoor plants, baking bread, sweeping, and dusting. Children under four-and-a-half years of age are naturally drawn toward these Practical Life exercises due to their "sensitive periods."[75] A sensitive period, often known as a

---

Oxford: Clio, 2004. Print. The Clio Montessori Ser. Pages 223-229.

[70] Ibid. Pages 182-188.

[71] Ibid.

[72] Montessori, Maria. *Creative Development in the Child.* Ed. Rukmini Ramachandran. Vol. 1. Chennai: Kalakshetra, 2007. Print. Pages 192-199, 206-207.

[73] Montessori, Maria. *Dr. Montessori's Own Handbook.* Mineola: Dover Publications, 2005. Print. Pages 90-96, 116-117.

[74] Montessori, Maria. *The Absorbent Mind.* Trans. Claude A. Claremont. Vol. 1. Oxford: Clio, 2004. Print. The Clio Montessori Ser. Pages 182-188, 190, 240-261.

[75] Montessori, Maria. *What You Should Know about Your Child.* Vol. 4. Amsterdam: Montessori-Pierson, 2008. Print. The Montessori Ser. Pages 9-11, 16-18, 34-37.

"critical period" or a "window of opportunity" in traditional education, is an intense motivation during a finite period of time in early childhood for performing certain tasks to promote optimal self-development. The four sensitive periods recognized by Montessorians for children under the age of six are order, movement, refinement of sensory perception, and language. All sensitive periods, with the exception of language, are most intense when a child is under four-and-a-half years of age. Around four-and-a-half years of age, the sensitive periods for order, movement, and the refinement of sensory perception begin to diminish or disappear.[76] Language remains an intense motivation through the age of six.[77] Because sensitive periods disappear at such an early age, it is essential that young children be provided an array of Practical Life exercises both at school and in the home for their holistic development. Keep in mind that while these sensitive periods are at work, the child will likely be more interested in the process of completing a sequence of actions rather than its outcome. A young child who washes a table, for example, does not wash the table to clean it. Instead, the young table washer is fulfilling an inner directive to exercise, improve, and master his gross and fine motor coordination so that he may accomplish more complex tasks, both physical and intellectual, in the future.[78] Do not be alarmed if your child repeats Practical Life tasks[79] fifty or more times in succession[80] while showing signs of

[76] Montessori, Maria. *The Discovery of the Child.* Trans. Mary A. Johnstone. Madras: Kalakshetra, 2006. Print. Pages 244-245.

[77] Ibid. Page 292.

[78] Montessori, Maria. *Creative Development in the Child.* Ed. Rukmini Ramachandran. Vol. 1. Chennai: Kalakshetra, 2007. Print. Pages 54-68, 73-75, 89-101, 108, 154-159.

[79] Ibid. Pages 52-59.

profound concentration such as an intense stare or pouty face.[81] This is an important developmental stage wherein the child is constructing his mind to conquer future challenges as a basis for all intellectual development including preparation for mathematics.[82] Whenever possible, allow the child to concentrate upon hands-on, purposeful Practical Life tasks without interruption. Praise or commentary, no matter how subtle, can easily break a child's concentration[83] which can lead to agitation and possibly behavior problems if persistent interruptions continue over the long term.[84] In the Casa, concentration upon purposeful work is protected by the three hour uninterrupted work period as well as rules that prevent working students from interruption except during transition times or an emergency. While a three hour uninterrupted work period may not be suitable for your particular circumstances at home, make an effort to provide a calm, prepared environment that protects your child's holistic, developmentally important activities whenever possible. Taking the time to create a prepared home environment with Practical Life activities that encourage concentration, repetition, and normalization help pave the way for your child's future mathematic experiences.[85]

---

[80] Montessori, Maria. *The Advanced Montessori Method I*. Vol. 9. Oxford: Clio, 2004. Print. The Clio Montessori Ser. Pages 69-75, 117-131.

[81] Montessori, Maria. *The Secret of Childhood*. Trans. Barbara B. Carter. Hyderabad: Orient Longman, 2006. Print. Pages 124-126.

[82] Montessori, Maria. *Dr. Montessori's Own Handbook*. Mineola: Dover Publications, 2005. Print. Pages 91-95.

[83] Montessori, Maria. *The Absorbent Mind*. Trans. Claude A. Claremont. Vol. 1. Oxford: Clio, 2004. Print. The Clio Montessori Ser. Pages 255-256.

[84] Montessori, Maria. *The Child, Society and the World: Unpublished Speeches and Writings*. Vol. 7. Oxford: Clio, 2006. Print. The Clio Montessori Ser. Pages 6-9, 15-16.

[85] Montessori, Maria. *What You Should Know about Your Child*. Vol. 4.

• Provide knobbed puzzles, shape sorting toys, memory tiles, and other activities that emphasize 1:1 correspondence, the simple mathematical task of matching an object to its corresponding item. Once your child is experienced with pairing, or matching, introduce toys that allow grading, the organization of materials in a logical sequence according to a given sensorial quality. Unpainted, metric, wooden building blocks in various sizes can be arranged from large to small, thick to thin, or long to short depending upon the dimensions of the blocks. Other grading activities that can be explored at home include arranging cans in the kitchen from short to tall, organizing fabric swatches of a single color from light to dark, as well as taking apart and reassembling nesting dolls.

• To stock your home environment with developmentally appropriate Practical Life and Sensorial-inspired materials for your child's exploration and growth, visit Montessori Services at www.montessoriservices.com. Also check out Melissa & Doug at www.melissaanddoug.com. While not official AMI materials suppliers,[86] Montessori Services and Melissa & Doug offer many materials suitable for classroom and home use. Melissa & Doug, a toy company, produces hard-to-find classic toys such as wooden building blocks, knobbed puzzles, large beads for stringing, lacing exercises, and 1:1 correspondence activities that are well-made and attractive. These hands-on activities for your child's exploration aid his fine motor and intellectual development in preparation for future academic success.[87]

Amsterdam: Montessori-Pierson, 2008. Print. The Montessori Ser. Pages 9-11, 16-18, 34-43.

[86]Official material suppliers for AMI Montessori schools are listed on AMI/USA's website: https://amiusa.org/school-standards/.

[87] Montessori, Maria. *The Child in the Family*. Trans. Nancy R. Cirillo. Vol. 8.

Organization of Mathematics in the Casa

For organizational purposes, all official mathematics activities in the Casa are divided into six categories or groups. Each group focuses on a particular aspect of mathematics. Group 1: Numbers 1-10 introduces and reinforces the quantities "one" through "ten" as well as their corresponding numerical symbols. The concept of "zero" as a null or empty category is also explored. Group 2: The Decimal System highlights the decimal system categories from units through the thousands in both concrete and written notation. Practice with mathematics equations into the thousands often occurs during small group games called "Collective Exercises." Following group practice, students solve equations into the thousands individually with a material known as "The Stamp Game." Group 3: Continuation of Counting introduces and reinforces numbers beyond ten into the thousands through several hands-on activities using color-coded beads and number cards. Special emphasis is placed on teen numbers 11 – 19 to solidify student comprehension. Group 4: Memorization Work gives students the opportunity to manipulate color-coded materials in order to learn and further explore the four operations of mathematics: addition, subtraction, multiplication, and division. Group 5: Passage to Abstraction aids students on their journey from concrete to abstract mathematics. Complete passage to abstraction occurs when a child can accurately and confidently solve any mathematical equation on paper or mentally without the assistance of concrete materials. This level of expertise is highly dependent upon student readiness and may not occur until the child's early elementary years. Group 6: Fractions introduces the fractions "one whole" through "ten tenths" as well as simple fraction equations in the four operations of mathematics in preparation for Montessori Elementary studies.

Oxford: Clio, 2006. Print. The Clio Montessori Ser. Pages 53-59.

Primary children are not aware of these six mathematic designations as they are designed to assist the guide in lesson planning rather than as a student rubric or checklist. For reference, descriptions of each of the six categories of mathematics presented in the Casa follow.

Group 1: Numbers 1-10

Manipulatives in Group 1: Numbers 1-10 help children discover how quantities and numbers are used to determine how many of a given set of objects exist. While many children are able to count to ten and recognize their corresponding numerical symbols before they enter the Casa, exercises in Group 1 concretely demonstrate the significance of quantities and numbers "one" through "ten." Even if a child comes to class with prior counting knowledge, all Group 1: Numbers 1-10 activities are introduced to ensure comprehension. It is important to remember that many young children who can allegedly count to ten are merely parroting a memorized sequence of numbers without understanding what they actually mean. Likewise, a child who can identify the printed numerals "1" through "10" may simply recognize their appearance at a superficial level rather than comprehend their meaning.

A solid understanding of the quantities "one" through "ten," including their corresponding numerical symbols "1" through "10," provides an essential foundation for all future mathematics studies.[88] As the foundation for all mathematics in the Casa, all Group 1: Numbers 1-10 activities must be completely mastered before a child may be introduced to further mathematics exercises. Once a child proves his mastery of Group 1: Numbers 1-10, the guide begins to introduce activities from other Montessori Primary mathematics categories including Group 2: The Decimal System.

---

[88] Montessori, Maria. *Creative Development in the Child.* Ed. Rukmini Ramachandran. Vol. 2. Chennai: Kalakshetra, 2007. Print. Pages 20-29.

Group 2: The Decimal System

Activities in Group 2: The Decimal System are based upon groups of ten. In the Casa, groups of ten are concretely illustrated with beads. Units are represented by single beads, tens by strings of ten beads, hundreds by squares of ten tens, and thousands by cubes of ten hundreds. This arrangement of quantities demonstrates how ten of any category becomes one of the next higher category. Ten single units, for example, become a ten. Likewise, ten tens become a hundred and ten hundreds become a thousand. Students also continue to explore the importance of "0" as a placeholder for empty decimal system categories. By working with these hands-on materials, children learn the relationships between and among the decimal system categories without the use of tedious drills or standardized tests.

Unlike Group 1: Numbers 1-10, which must be completely mastered before receiving presentations from other mathematics groups, Group 2: The Decimal System is introduced parallel to mathematics presentations in Group 3: Continuation of Counting and Group 4: Memorization Work. Activities in Groups 2 through 4 are not strictly sequential, meaning that children receive presentations from each of these groups around the same time. Keep in mind the parallel nature of mathematical Groups 2 through 4 as you read this article.

Group 3: Continuation of Counting

Group 3: Continuation of Counting explores the names of quantities beyond "ten" into the thousands as well as their recursive sequence. Through hands-on manipulation of Group 3 activities, children discover that all real numbers in our recursive sequence of counting, no matter how large the number, use only the numerals "0" through "9." Color-coded beads and cards are used in Group 3: Continuation of Counting activities for clarity and to appeal to a young child's sense of classification. Like Group 2: The Decimal System, Group 3: Continuation of Counting exercises are presented parallel to activities in Group 2 and Group 4: Memorization Work.

Group 4: Memorization Work

Essential combinations of mathematical operations and their accurate calculation are the emphasis of Group 4: Memorization Work. An "essential combination" is a mathematical equation with three integers in which two or more of those integers are nine or less than nine. Through the concrete materials in Group 4, children discover and memorize the essential combinations of all four operations of mathematics. For example, if a child learns all the essential combinations of addition from $1 + 1 = 2$ through $9 + 9 = 18$, he can eventually solve any addition problem on paper or mentally. The child also learns the essential combinations of subtraction from $18 - 9 = 9$ through $1 - 1 = 0$, as well as the essential combinations of multiplication ($1 \times 1 = 1$ through $9 \times 9 = 81$) and the essential combinations of division ($81 \div 9 = 9$ through $1 \div 1 = 1$). Keep in mind that Group 4: Memorization Work is not necessarily sequential. Activities from Group 4: Memorization Work are presented parallel to exercises in Group 2: The Decimal System and Group 3: Continuation of Counting.

Group 5: Passage to Abstraction

In Group 5: Passage to Abstraction, a child's previously acquired mathematics knowledge is applied to complex exercises which have few concrete manipulatives. The guide's task in Group 5 is to observe for opportunities to facilitate a child's transition from concrete to abstract mathematics. Although materials such as "The Small Bead Frame," a manipulative similar to an abacus, are used to assist a child transitioning from hands-on mathematics to mathematics completed solely on paper or mentally, materials other than paper and pencil will eventually become unnecessary to solve problems. Exactly when an individual child no longer requires mathematics manipulatives to accurately complete calculations varies. Assuming a proper foundation in mathematics has been provided, complete passage to abstraction generally occurs when a child is about to graduate from the Casa or early in his Montessori Elementary years, around age six or seven. As a developmental occurrence, complete passage to abstraction cannot be forced or rushed. The adult can merely provide guided exposure to the necessary, hands-on manipulatives to assist the child's transition. Ultimately, only the child's individual path of development can determine when he will be ready to replace hands-on materials with pencil and paper, followed by mental calculation.

Group 6: Fractions

Group 6: Fractions is the only mathematics area in the Casa which concerns numbers less than one. Due to their abstract nature, fractions are among the last materials presented in the Casa. Students in the Primary Casa's prepared environment learn the fractions "one whole" through "ten tenths" as well as how to solve simple fraction equations in the four operations of mathematics including division. Mixed fractions, improper fractions, and reduction to the lowest common denominator are typically not introduced until the child's Montessori Elementary education begins around the age of six or seven. Once in Montessori Elementary, the child continues his study of fractions from where the Primary curriculum left off.

The Five Step Model of Instruction and Exploration

The six mathematical categories in the Casa (Numbers 1-10,

The Decimal System, Continuation of Counting, Memorization Work, Passage to Abstraction, and Fractions) are further divided into a five step model of instruction and exploration for maximum clarity and effectiveness. These steps are Introduction to Quantity, Introduction to Symbol, Association between Quantity and Symbol, Practice, and The Test (Verification). Like the six groups of mathematics, children in the Casa are unaware of these five steps as they are designed exclusively for the guide's lesson planning. For reference, a summary of the five step model of instruction and exploration of mathematics manipulatives in the Casa follows.

Step 1: Introduction to Quantity

In the Casa, experience almost always precedes language. In order to best understand and remember an idea, a young child must first experience a concept in its concrete form using one or more of his five senses in accordance with his sensitive periods.[89] Recall the four sensitive periods recognized by Montessorians: order, movement, refinement of sensory perception, and language. Although order, movement, and refinement of sensory perception are typically most intense before a child reaches four-and-a-half years of age,[90] children under the age of six are still concrete sensorial learners rather than rational abstract thinkers.[91] For this reason, the guide presents the concrete representation of a given quantity long before introducing its corresponding numerical symbol. Numerical symbols are only introduced in the Casa following adequate hands-on experience with the physical

---

[89] Montessori, Maria. *Dr. Montessori's Own Handbook*. Mineola: Dover Publications, 2005. Print. Pages 79-87.

[90] Montessori, Maria. *The Discovery of the Child*. Trans. Mary A. Johnstone. Madras: Kalakshetra, 2006. Print. Pages 244-245.

[91] Montessori, Maria. *Creative Development in the Child*. Ed. Rukmini Ramachandran. Vol. 1. Chennai: Kalakshetra, 2007. Print. Pages 222-229, 233.

quantity.

An example of Step 1: Introduction to Quantity as applied to Group 1: Numbers 1-10 is the initial Number Rods presentation. During the first Number Rods lesson, the child learns the quantities "one" through "ten" by touching each segment of each Number Rod with the palm of his hand. The names of the quantities are introduced using the Three Period Lesson: Naming, Recognition, and Remembering. Three sequential Number Rods are introduced at a time starting with "one." Unless the child experiences great difficulty with the work, all quantities "one" through "ten" can be introduced over the course of two days or a week. Extensions of the Second and Third Periods may be presented for review.

Step 2: Introduction to Symbol

Once a child has had experience with the interactive presentation for Step 1: Introduction to Quantity, he learns the activity's corresponding numerical symbols through Step 2: Introduction to Symbol. In alignment with a young child's sensorial acquisition of learning, numerical symbols are introduced in isolation using hands-on manipulatives. Like quantities, numerical symbols are introduced using the Three Period Lesson. Typically, up to six written numerical symbols can be introduced per day depending upon interest and readiness, although there are exceptions to this limitation. Teen numbers, for example, may be presented in a single day if the child is confident or has prior knowledge. The guide paces Three Period Lessons according to her observations of the individual student's needs and interests.

Step 2: Introduction to Symbol is applied in Group 1: Numbers 1-10 through the "Sandpaper Numerals." Numerical symbols "0" through "9" are cut from sandpaper and mounted on wooden boards for tactile exploration. Typically over the course of two days to a week, the child learns the symbols "0" through "9" via Three Period Lessons. Only the symbols "0" through "9" are introduced with the Sandpaper Numerals as these symbols can be used to transcribe any real number regardless of size. There is no need to introduce "10" as a separate Sandpaper Numeral because "10" is composed of a "1" and a "0." If the child already knows the numbers before the official Sandpaper Numerals presentation, the guide emphasizes tracing the numbers to solidify the student's knowledge and to provide a foundation for future legible handwriting. Extensions of the Second and Third Periods may be presented for review.

Step 3: Association between Quantity and Symbol

Following hands-on experience with quantities and numerical symbols in isolation, the two qualities are combined in Step 3: Association between Quantity and Symbol. This combination of quantities and their corresponding numerical symbols demonstrates the direct relationship between these two aspects of mathematics in a manner that is clear to children under the age of six or seven.[92]

Step 3: Association between Quantity and Symbol is applied in Group 1: Numbers 1-10 during the presentation "Number Rods and Cards." Once the child understands the quantities "one" through "ten" with the Number Rods as well as the numerical symbols "0" through "9" with the Sandpaper Numerals, he can effectively combine quantities and symbols by labeling the Number Rods with their corresponding wooden number cards. Since the child is already familiar with the numbers "1" and "0," it is usually not difficult for the child to recognize "10" with some help from the guide. By working with Number Rods and Cards as well as their related activities, the child practices and mentally solidifies the connection between quantities and symbols to heighten his comprehension in preparation for future mathematics work. Extensions of the Second and Third Periods related to Step

---

[92] Montessori, Maria. *Dr. Montessori's Own Handbook*. Mineola: Dover Publications, 2005. Print. Pages 119-126.

3: Association between Quantity and Symbol are presented and practiced for further experience and mental refinement.

Step 4: Practice

Once a child successfully establishes the connection between quantities and their corresponding numerical symbols during Step 3: Association between Quantity and Symbol, activities are introduced which allow the child to further practice, explore, and solidify his newfound understanding of a given aspect of mathematics. This category of mathematical exploration is aptly named "Step 4: Practice."

To help keep children engaged while simultaneously encouraging practice, there is often more than one material that highlights the same skill. In Group 1: Numbers 1-10, there are two practice activities: "Spindle Boxes" and "Cards and Counters." Spindle Boxes allow a child to place bundles of dowels or spindles into compartments labeled with the numerical symbols "0" through "9." The compartment labeled "0" remains empty as a reminder that "zero" represents a null or empty category. Cards and Counters are designed for matching loose quantities represented by round disks, or "counters," to their corresponding numerical symbols written on wooden number cards. Both exercises help students continue their explorations of quantities and symbols "0" through "10" to perfect their comprehension.

Step 5: The Test (Verification)

In the Montessori Casa, Step 5: The Test celebrates the child's newfound mathematical knowledge rather than drawing attention to his mistakes or lack of comprehension. In alignment with a young child's hands-on mode of learning, mathematics tests in the Casa are not conducted on paper or graded. Instead, the guide assesses a student's knowledge by presenting a fun exercise or activity that incorporates the child's prior mathematical experiences in a given area. If a child struggles with any part of the verification activity, the guide uses her observations of the student's performance as a guideline for re-introducing areas of concern as needed before presenting new material. Keep in mind that children in the Casa are never made aware of the fact that they are being tested. As far as the students are concerned, the guide is playing an interesting new game. This natural, holistic, age-appropriate assessment technique helps the guide determine the extent of an individual student's mathematical knowledge without the stressful pressure of standardized tests or the humiliation of receiving red marks on a paper for poor performance.

Following mastery of Step 4: Practice exercises in Group 1: Numbers 1-10, the guide introduces Step 5: The Test (Verification) through "The Memory Game of Numbers." As mentioned earlier in this article, The Memory Game of Numbers consists of number slips labeled from "0" to "10" placed in a bag, basket, or on a dish. Each child playing The Memory Game of Numbers draws a slip and remembers his number. When it is his turn, he is asked to bring his number of "something" in the room back to the rug. If these directions are too vague for a new player, the guide can simplify the activity by asking the child to bring his number of like objects to the rug. For instance, the guide may say, "Bring your number of buttons to the rug." If the child can consistently retrieve the correct number of objects that match his slip over the course of several rounds played over a period of several days, the guide knows that he understands what written numerical symbols represent. If the child constantly makes mistakes or is bewildered by the gameplay, the guide helps the child build his comprehension through continued practice with previous mathematics exercises in Group 1: Numbers 1-10. There is never any shame involved in extra practice with earlier presented materials. In fact, in Montessori schools with both Primary and Elementary programs, it is not uncommon for Montessori Elementary children to borrow

Primary mathematics materials such as the Number Rods as a concrete review to help aid further mathematic exploration.[93] Likewise, advanced Primary students in a high-functioning Montessori prepared environment may borrow Montessori Elementary materials at the guide's discretion if he exhausts the possibilities of Primary mathematics manipulatives.[94] In the child-centered, non-competitive atmosphere of the Casa, children are at liberty to learn at their own pace without having to worry about outpacing or keeping up with their peers.[95] Regardless of the child's current level of mathematical expertise, the guide is there to assist him in his ongoing quest for knowledge and lifelong learning as its own reward.[96]

Conclusion

Following mastery of Group 1: Numbers 1-10, the guide presents a vast array of sequential and parallel mathematics lessons related to the decimal system, numbers greater than ten, and the four operations of mathematics (addition, subtraction, multiplication, and division). Newfound skills in mathematics are reinforced through several practice activities including group games, individual "Practice Charts," and "Word Problems." Every mathematics presentation is presented lovingly at an age-appropriate level, making mathematics both enjoyable and understandable. With a solid foundation in the Montessori Primary Casa, a child is well-prepared for increasingly complex mathematical challenges that await him in the future.

---

[93] Montessori, Maria. *The Child, Society and the World: Unpublished Speeches and Writings*. Vol. 7. Oxford: Clio, 2006. Print. The Clio Montessori Ser. Pages 68-69.

[94] Montessori, Maria. *The Absorbent Mind*. Trans. Claude A. Claremont. Vol. 1. Oxford: Clio, 2004. Print. The Clio Montessori Ser. Pages 205-207.

[95] Ibid. Pages 206-207.

[96] Montessori, Maria. *The Secret of Childhood*. Trans. Barbara B. Carter. Hyderabad: Orient Longman, 2006. Print. Pages 146-148.

References

Da Prato, Mary. *Montessori Primary Addition*. Seattle: CreateSpace Independent Publishing Platform, 2017. Print.

Da Prato, Mary. *My First Montessori Book of Quantities*. 2nd ed. Seattle: CreateSpace Independent Publishing Platform, 2014. Print.

Montessori, Maria. *The Absorbent Mind*. Trans. Claude A. Claremont. Vol. 1. Oxford: Clio, 2004. Print. The Clio Montessori Ser.

Montessori, Maria. *The Advanced Montessori Method I*. Vol. 9. Oxford: Clio, 2004. Print. The Clio Montessori Ser.

Montessori, Maria. *The California Lectures of Maria Montessori, 1915: Collected Speeches and Writings*. Ed. Robert G. Buckenmeyer. Vol. 15. Oxford: Clio, 2000. Print. The Clio Montessori Ser.

Montessori, Maria. *The Child in the Family*. Trans. Nancy R. Cirillo. Vol. 8. Oxford: Clio, 2006. Print. The Clio Montessori Ser.

Montessori, Maria. *The Child, Society and the World: Unpublished Speeches and Writings*. Vol. 7. Oxford: Clio, 2006. Print. The Clio Montessori Ser.

Montessori, Maria. *Creative Development in the Child*. Ed. Rukmini Ramachandran. Vol. 1. Chennai: Kalakshetra, 2007. Print.

Montessori, Maria. *Creative Development in the Child*. Ed. Rukmini Ramachandran. Vol. 2. Chennai: Kalakshetra, 2007. Print.

Montessori, Maria. *The Discovery of the Child*. Trans. Mary A. Johnstone. Madras: Kalakshetra, 2006. Print.

Montessori, Maria. *Dr. Montessori's Own Handbook*. Mineola: Dover Publications, 2005. Print.

Montessori, Maria. *The Secret of Childhood*. Trans. Barbara B. Carter. Hyderabad: Orient Longman, 2006. Print.

Montessori, Maria. *What You Should Know about Your Child*. Vol. 4. Amsterdam: Montessori-Pierson, 2008. Print. The Montessori Ser.

"Standards for AMI Montessori Classrooms." *AMI/USA*. AMI/USA, 2014. Web. 18 Apr. 2018. <https://amiusa.org/school-standards/>.

ANIMALS IN CHILDREN'S LITERATURE:
A MONTESSORI APPROACH

From *The Tale of Peter Rabbit* to *A Bear Called Paddington*, anthropomorphic animals who speak and dress like people have been largely an unquestioned staple of children's literature for generations. But what if fanciful stories of clothed rabbits pilfering parsley and bears bumbling through train stations were not in the best psychological interest of their intended audience? What if, instead of behaving like humans, animals in children's literature were expected to behave like animals and were cherished for doing so? Welcome to Montessori's philosophy of reality-based fiction for young children.

One of the first female physicians in Italy, Dr. Maria Montessori developed a child-centered method of education in 1907,[97] and continued to refine her scientific pedagogy until her death in 1952.[98] By attentively observing children over the course of several decades, Dr. Montessori made a number of extraordinary discoveries regarding the needs and interests of children. Among her numerous observations was the shocking discovery that children under six or seven years of age actually preferred realistic fiction to works of fantasy if given a choice. To her surprise, young students permitted to follow their own interests often rejected fanciful stories outright by walking away from an adult storyteller to find a more suitable occupation. The subject of fanciful versus realistic tales for children is a topic Dr. Montessori discussed at length in a number of her books and speeches, perhaps most notably during a lecture entitled "Truth and Fairy Tales" which can be read in *The 1946 London Lectures*.[99]

---

[97] Helfrich, M. Shannon. *Montessori Learning in the 21ˢᵗ Century: A Guide for Parents & Teachers*. Troutdale: NewSage Press, 2011. Print. Pages 8-12.

[98] Lillard, Paula P. *Montessori Today: A Comprehensive Approach to Education from Birth to Adulthood*. New York: Schocken, 1996. Print. Page 152.

The assertion that fantasy and fairy tales, which often include talking animals, are inappropriate for young children is a controversial claim both in Dr. Montessori's time and today. Adults often fondly recall the bedtime stories of their youth, replete with fiery dragons, fairy princesses, and talking pigs among other colorful characters. Some might argue, "Who was Dr. Montessori to rob children of these comforting experiences? I grew up on a steady diet of children's classics, and talking animals never did me any harm!" But this essay does not intend to discredit anyone's warm childhood memories, nor does it intend to defend current early childhood development practice when it comes to defining quality children's literature. Instead, this essay is designed to explain the Montessori approach to selecting appropriate children's literature in accordance with Dr. Montessori's scientific observations and discoveries which are just as relevant today as they were over one hundred years ago.[100]

It is vital to understand that the Montessori Method does not represent a war against fantasy and the imagination. Rather, the Montessori Method is a philosophy of bringing each child to his fullest potential through hands-on, reality-based experiences, including hearing and reading fiction which portrays animals in a realistic manner. These reality-based experiences, not fantasy, lay an essential foundation for every young child's physical, intellectual, and emotional wellbeing.[101] And it is through the reading of realistic literature that the essential human quality of the imagination is truly kindled.[102]

---

[99] Montessori, Maria. *The 1946 London Lectures*. Ed. Annette Haines. Vol. 17. Amsterdam: Montessori-Pierson, 2012. Print. The Montessori Ser. Pages 187-192.

[100] Montessori, Maria. *The Child, Society, and the World: Unpublished Speeches and Writings*. Vol. 7. Oxford: Clio, 2006. Print. The Clio Montessori Ser. Page 74.

[101] Montessori, Maria. *The Advanced Montessori Method I*. Vol. 9. Oxford: Clio, 2004. Print. The Clio Montessori Ser. Pages 196-205.

What is the definition of "reality-based" literature? In the Montessori Primary classroom for children approximately two-and-a-half through six years of age, "reality-based" literature refers to any age-appropriate story which is accurate, plausible, free from political bias, and appeals to the interests and sensibilities of young children. Animal characters in reality-based literature only perform actions which are possible in real life. Unlike many popular animal characters in fanciful children's literature, animals in reality-based literature do not possess human speech, engage in exclusively human activities such as wearing clothes, perform tasks impossible to the species such as managing a mission to Mars, or appear in fanciful colors not seen in nature. Reality-based literature in Montessori is also screened for age-appropriateness. For example, disturbing topics such as elephants being hunted for ivory, although an unfortunate reality, are not suitable for the age group and are therefore not presented in a classroom for young children. In addition to its aforementioned attributes, reality-based literature for children is also expected to uphold high literary and artistic standards to promote optimal language development and art appreciation. Although picture book illustrations do not need to be technical, they should not be overly cartoonish or gaudy.

But why must children's books be reality-based? Besides realistic fiction being naturally more appealing to young children than fantasy,[103] reality-based books provide a necessary balance to our often fantasy-obsessed culture. There is no lack of fanciful imagery for readers of all ages in the world outside the Montessori classroom. Look in the picture book section of your local library, and you will quickly find a multitude of books which feature talking animals who get dressed, go to school, and solve problems

---

[102] Montessori, Maria. *The Advanced Montessori Method II*. Vol. 13. Oxford: Clio, 2006. Print. The Clio Montessori Ser. Pages 196-202.

[103] Montessori, Maria. *The 1946 London Lectures*. Ed. Annette Haines. Vol. 17. Amsterdam: Montessori-Pierson, 2012. Print. The Montessori Ser. Pages 187-192.

like humans. It is clear that young children are not being denied fantasy in the wider world despite their reality-based literature experiences in the Montessori Primary prepared environment. Perhaps fantasy should be kept to a minimum, especially when children under six years of age are concerned. Keep in mind that children under approximately seven years of age typically lack a reasoning mind.[104] While every child is different, a lack of reasoning ability makes it difficult for many young children to distinguish fantasy from reality.[105] So why confuse them with fantastical images of talking elephants and purple zebras? It is far better to provide books which feature real elephants and zebras, especially if young students have never seen these animals in real life. Moreover, when children in our world are inundated with fantasy, it is easy to forget the simple appeal of reality. To a three year old child, a charming story about a robin eating worms in the backyard is extremely fascinating. Young children are highly curious and eager to learn about the world around them.[106] [107] If they are offered a steady diet of mice singing operettas, how are they supposed to gain an appreciation of real mice scurrying to and fro, gathering food while being mindful of potential dangers? As Douglas Adams, the late science fiction author, so aptly put it, "Isn't it enough to see that a garden is beautiful without having to believe that there are fairies at the bottom of it too?"

Before decrying reality-based children's literature as somehow

---

[104] Montessori, Maria. *The Absorbent Mind*. Trans. Claude A. Claremont. Vol. 1. Oxford: Clio, 2004. Print. The Clio Montessori Ser. Pages 175-177, 190.

[105] American Friends of Tel Aviv University. "Fantasy-Reality Confusion a Primary Cause of Childhood Nighttime Fears." ScienceDaily. ScienceDaily, 13 Nov. 2012. Web. 15 Mar. 2017.
<www.sciencedaily.com/releases/2012/11/121113134926.htm>.

[106] Montessori, Maria. *The Advanced Montessori Method I*. Vol. 9. Oxford: Clio, 2004. Print. The Clio Montessori Ser. Pages 151-175, 196- 204, 228, 232-233.

[107] Montessori, Maria. *Creative Development in the Child*. Ed. Rukmini Ramachandran. Vol. 1. Chennai: Kalakshetra, 2007. Print. Pages 222-223.

inferior to fantasy, ask yourself why a children's book author or illustrator would choose to write a story about anthropomorphic animals in the place of human characters. Why must a story about a child being apprehensive about his first day of school star an anthropomorphic turtle instead of a human child, which would be far more sensible and appropriate for the story? Did the author or publisher think that a child would find reading about another child his age too boring to print? This hardly seems the case, as there are many picture books about human children enjoying life and overcoming challenges. Or is it perhaps that authors or publishers erroneously believe that animals exhibiting their natural behaviors are too boring for children to read about? In an odd fashion, portraying animals as human substitutes could be regarded as somewhat insulting to the animal protagonists who have been anthropomorphized. Are we so wonderful as a species that every animal in a children's picture book must think and act exactly like us? Is it not enough for an animal protagonist to behave as nature intended, or must we impose our human values, behaviors, and societal norms onto that character to make him somehow more relatable to us? None of this is to suggest that an animal must never be portrayed in a fanciful manner. Nor should this be regarded as a condemnation of beloved children's classics such as *The Tale of Peter Rabbit* and *Curious George*. Instead, it is an invitation to carefully consider why our bookshelves for children are inundated with fanciful tales of animals when there are so many fascinating animal stories that can be told without resorting to unnecessary anthropomorphism.

After sifting through the extensive and stringent criteria for reality-based children's literature, it can be challenging to find books which follow the rules for a Montessori Primary classroom. It is especially difficult to find fictional picture books starring appealing animal protagonists which do not feature anthropomorphism. Thankfully, there are a few books of note which meet Montessori's reality-based criteria, feature animal protagonists, and provide a delightful literary experience for children under the age of seven. The first example concerns a trilogy of books by Marjorie Flack which feature a Scottie dog as the protagonist: *Angus and the Ducks*, *Angus and the Cat*, and *Angus Lost*. Each of the three books in this series follows Angus's charmingly realistic adventures as he learns how to navigate his world. Without speaking, wearing clothes, or otherwise adopting human behaviors, Angus manages to delight readers as he explores, chases ducks, gradually befriends a housecat, and becomes lost in a cave during a blizzard. Unlike so many animal protagonists in picture books, Angus has the freedom to behave as a lovable dog rather than an anthropomorphized version of a dog. He is not unnecessarily cast as a substitute for a role that would be better suited to a human character. Instead, through his realistic actions, Angus is able to express a wide range of emotions including curiosity, fear, loneliness, and joy in a manner natural to his species while still instilling a sense of empathy and enchantment in the young reader. Much of Angus's emotional state is portrayed through Marjorie Flack's delightfully straightforward illustrations. Instead of making comments the way a human would, Angus reveals his feelings to the reader through his credible expressions and postures. Angus's illustrated actions and emotions are reinforced by the reality-based text. It is not necessary for Angus to behave like a human in order to make his story interesting. If anything, the charm and appeal of Angus's antics would be diminished if he were to suddenly step out of character and say, just as a human would, "Hello there, ducks. And how are you today?" Since Angus's adventures are grounded in reality rather than fantasy, young children are able to enjoy the story without casting unnecessary human projections upon it. The reader's empathy for Angus stems not from him behaving like a human trapped in an animal body, but from Angus acting as a fully-realized animal character with a range of relatable actions and emotions despite being a member of a different species.

Another reality-based animal story of note is Clare Turlay Newberry's *Marshmallow*, winner of a Caldecott Honor in 1943. This picture book concerns the adoption of a young white rabbit, the titular Marshmallow, into a home that already has a cat, Oliver. The book follows Oliver's gradual acceptance of another pet in his home while Marshmallow simultaneously adapts to living away from his mother. This wonderfully touching story is told without either animal ever speaking a word. Like Marjorie Flack's stories about Angus, Clare Turlay Newberry's portrayal of realistic animals in *Marshmallow* is more than sufficient to entertain and evoke empathy in the young reader. When Marshmallow first arrives at his new home, it is perfectly clear that he is frightened and apprehensive. It is also perfectly clear that Oliver is uneasy and jealous at the arrival of a new animal invading his territory. Gradually, the two animal characters, although different species, befriend one another, resulting in a happy ending to a warm story. All this is accomplished not by artificially forcing animal characters to behave according to human norms but by allowing animal protagonists to behave according to the norms of their respective species. If Clare Turlay Newberry had made the decision to anthropomorphize Oliver and Marshmallow, the core essence of the story would have been irreparably lost.

Additional reality-based children's stories about animals include *Big Red Barn* by Margaret Wise Brown, *Bonny's Big Day* by James Herriot, *Granite* by Susan Butcher and David Monson, *Kamik: An Inuit Puppy Story* by Donald Uluadluak, *Kamik's First Sled* by Matilda Sulurayok, *Kamik Joins the Pack* by Darryl Baker, *A Kitten's Year* by Nancy Raines Day, and *Where is that Cat?* by Carol Greene as well as my own picture book, *Thomas the Squirrel*. All these fictional picture books for children, which were published by a variety authors in various years, share the common theme of permitting animal protagonists to exhibit their realistic behaviors and inclinations rather than miming human behaviors. These books and others like them, especially timeless classics like

Big Red Barn, stand as evidence that young children do not require animal protagonists in stories to act like people in order to make the stories enjoyable and relatable. It could be argued that a greater degree of respect and empathy is granted to picture books which demonstrate that animal protagonists are well-rounded and interesting enough in their own right to be the focus of their own stories. In contrast, putting picture book animals in exclusively human situations by dressing them up and making them speak could potentially send the inadvertent message to young children that animal characters are not interesting enough to appear in fiction in their natural form. A story about a baby elephant losing sight of his mother and finding her again in the last scene, for example, is more than sufficient to evoke children's empathy and maintain their interest providing the story is well-told and beautifully illustrated. There is no need to clutter a tender, well-executed animal story by forcing unrealistic actions and dialogue into the mix. In short, animal protagonists in picture books should be free to be the animals that they are, not the pseudo-humans children's authors often force them to be.

Although the criteria for reality-based children's stories in the Montessori Primary curriculum is excellent for children under six or seven years of age, the criteria for animal stories changes in accordance with the universal needs of children ages six or seven through twelve in the Montessori Elementary curriculum. Around the age of seven, children develop the ability to reason, an ability generally absent at a younger age.[108] In response to an elementary-aged child's psychological transformation from purely concrete to increasingly abstract thinking,[109] fanciful reading materials may be officially offered for the first time. *Aesop's Fables*, which would have been too abstract, incomprehensible, and dull for most

---

[108] Montessori, Maria. *The Absorbent Mind*. Trans. Claude A. Claremont. Vol. 1. Oxford: Clio, 2004. Print. The Clio Montessori Ser. Pages 175-177, 190.
[109] Montessori, Maria. *Creative Development in the Child*. Ed. Rukmini Ramachandran. Vol. 1. Chennai: Kalakshetra, 2007. Print. Pages 222-229.

children under six or seven years of age,[110] may suddenly pique an elementary child's keen interest in cultivating his imagination to its fullest extent.[111] Works of high-quality literary fiction featuring animal protagonists, such as *Charlotte's Web* and *Black Beauty*, may also be introduced around this age. Now that the child is older and possesses greater cognitive maturity,[112] he is finally able to fully enjoy stories which stretch the powers of imagination.[113] This is not to say that the Montessori Elementary child never reads reality-based literature as he did at a younger age. On the contrary, Dr. Montessori found that older children, while more receptive to fantasy than their younger counterparts,[114] generally still preferred realistic fiction when given the choice.[115] The difference between presenting talking animals to preschool-aged children and elementary-aged children is that the cognitive level of the older child is better suited to comprehend and enjoy fanciful tales than their younger peers who often cannot distinguish fantasy from reality.[116] It is also important to note that fanciful animal stories in the Montessori Elementary classroom are still expected to represent high literary quality. In the Newbery Honor Book

---

[110] Montessori, Maria. *The 1946 London Lectures*. Ed. Annette Haines. Vol. 17. Amsterdam: Montessori-Pierson, 2012. Print. The Montessori Ser. Pages 187-192.

[111] Montessori, Maria. *To Educate the Human Potential*. Vol. 6. Oxford: Clio, 2003. Print. The Clio Montessori Ser. Pages 1-11.

[112] Montessori, Maria. *Creative Development in the Child*. Ed. Rukmini Ramachandran. Vol. 1. Chennai: Kalakshetra, 2007. Print. Pages 222-229.

[113] Montessori, Maria. *The 1946 London Lectures*. Ed. Annette Haines. Vol. 17. Amsterdam: Montessori-Pierson, 2012. Print. The Montessori Ser. Pages 187-192.

[114] Ibid. Pages 187-192.

[115] Montessori, Maria. *The Advanced Montessori Method II*. Vol. 13. Oxford: Clio, 2006. Print. The Clio Montessori Ser. Pages 198-202.

[116] American Friends of Tel Aviv University. "Fantasy-Reality Confusion a Primary Cause of Childhood Nighttime Fears." ScienceDaily. ScienceDaily, 13 Nov. 2012. Web. 15 Mar. 2017. <www.sciencedaily.com/releases/2012/11/121113134926.htm>.

Charlotte's Web, for example, animal characters speak like humans, but their patterns of behavior and subjects of concern are suited to the plot. Wilbur, the pig, walks on all fours as he explores the barnyard. The titular Charlotte, a spider, spins her web in the doorway of a barn. Even though Charlotte spinning words in her web to save Wilbur from being eaten is obviously a work of fantasy, this core element of the plot works because of its plausibility within the context of the overarching story. An elementary-aged child with a reasoning mind and imagination can easily make the cognitive leap from realistic farm animal behaviors to a fanciful story in which farm animal behaviors *seem* realistic enough to be believable. In *Charlotte's Web*, there is a clear reason why the main characters need to be animals, even though there are also human side characters. The animals propel the story because Wilbur's main concern is not to be eaten by humans, and his spider friend, Charlotte, enacts a plan to prevent this horrific fate. Talking animal characters and a bit of whimsy are essential in order for the author to make the story function. This is in sharp contrast to the plethora of children's picture books in which anthropomorphized animals behave exactly like humans to the point where it becomes pointless for animal characters to have been chosen to tell the story in the first place!

Understanding Montessori's philosophy of reality-based literature for children under approximately seven years of age is an excellent starting point for crafting realistic animal stories. Besides ensuring animal protagonists in picture books do not speak, wear clothes, or perform tasks impossible for the species, how should an aspiring children's author craft an enjoyable, age-appropriate animal story? First, the animal protagonist itself must be considered. What type of animal will be featured in the picture book? Will the story be about a dog, a cat, a rabbit, a cockatoo, a bear, or a walrus? Maybe a more unusual animal such as a tapir or hyrax will be the protagonist. Whichever animal is ultimately chosen, it is important to do research. This is essential whether the picture book will be fiction, non-fiction, or a fictionalized version of a true account. Learn about the natural behaviors of the chosen species by reading books and watching nature documentaries. If possible, closely observe local wildlife from a safe and respectful distance. When observing animals either locally or on a nature program, be attentive to how they interact with the surrounding environment as well as other members of the species. What is the animal's diet? Does it have any predators? For the purposes of writing for young children, remember to keep potentially frightening situations to a minimum. A small animal can certainly experience fear if a hawk is spotted nearby, but this should not be the focus of the story so as not to upset young readers. Keep human predators, such as poachers, out of picture books entirely. Even though ivory poachers and big game hunters still exist in the 21st century, young children should not be burdened with such unsettling topics. Remember, reality-based books must be age-appropriate and free from agendas. For young children, the purpose of hearing or reading a story is to be immersed in the wonderful world of literature to support optimal language development, not to learn about the many problems that plague our planet.

Once an animal protagonist is chosen and thoroughly researched, it is time to create the animal's story. What sort of realistic adventure will the animal character experience? If the chosen animal is a domestic cat or dog, what might be a believable plot? In the case of Clare Turlay Newberry's *Marshmallow*, Oliver the cat must learn to share his home with a new pet, a small white rabbit. In *Angus and the Ducks* by Marjorie Flack, Angus the dog sneaks out of the house when the door is accidentally left open in order to explore a familiar park without his leash. Both of these stories are charming because of their plausibility. What delightfully realistic animal story will you tell? Within the confines of your chosen animal's natural abilities and inclinations as well as Montessori's criteria for reality-based children's literature, the decision is yours.

A good guideline for children's authors, whether writing for preschoolers or elementary children, is to consider whether or not it is essential for an animal protagonist to tell the story. If the story can be told just as easily with human characters, what is the point of casting dressed up, talking animals in those roles? Animals of all kinds have a variety of fascinating characteristics which can be used to effectively tell a story in a manner that appeals to children. Perhaps it is time to bring more of those stories to the foreground without tacking unnecessary human characteristics to compelling animal protagonists. After all, a story about a Scottie dog chasing ducks in the park is a fine story to tell. But kindly tell it without stuffing the poor dog into a suit and tie.

References

The Aesop for Children. New York: Barnes & Noble Books, 1993. Print.

American Friends of Tel Aviv University. "Fantasy-Reality Confusion a Primary Cause of Childhood Nighttime Fears." ScienceDaily. ScienceDaily, 13 Nov.2012. Web. 15 Mar. 2017. <www.sciencedaily.com/releases/2012/11/121113134926.htm>.

Baker, Darryl. *Kamik Joins the Pack*. Toronto: Inhabit Media, 2016. Print.

Bond, Michael. *A Bear Called Paddington*. Boston: Houghton Mifflin Company, 1986. Print.

Brown, Margaret W. *Big Red Barn*. New York: HarperCollins Publishers, 1989. Print.

Butcher, Susan and David Monson. *Granite*. Fairbanks: Trail Breaker Kennel, 2008. Print.

Da Prato, Mary. *Thomas the Squirrel*. Seattle: CreateSpace Independent Publishing Platform, 2013. Print.

Day, Nancy R. *A Kitten's Year*. New York: HarperCollins Publishers, 2000. Print.

Flack, Marjorie. *Angus and the Cat*. New York: Doubleday, Doran & Company, Inc., 1931. Print.

Flack, Marjorie. *Angus and the Ducks*. New York: Doubleday, Doran & Company, Inc., 1930. Print.

Flack, Marjorie. *Angus Lost*. New York: Doubleday, Doran & Company, Inc., 1932. Print.

Greene, Carol. *Where Is That Cat?*. New York: Hyperion, 1999. Print.

Helfrich, M. Shannon. *Montessori Learning in the 21st Century: A Guide for Parents & Teachers*. Troutdale: NewSage Press, 2011. Print.

Herriot, James. *Bonny's Big Day*. New York: St. Martin's Press, 1987. Print.

Lillard, Paula P. *Montessori Today: A Comprehensive Approach to Education from Birth to Adulthood*. New York: Schocken, 1996. Print.

Montessori, Maria. *The 1946 London Lectures*. Ed. Annette Haines. Vol. 17. Amsterdam: Montessori-Pierson, 2012. Print. The Montessori Ser.

Montessori, Maria. *The Absorbent Mind*. Trans. Claude A. Claremont. Vol. 1. Oxford: Clio, 2004. Print. The Clio Montessori Ser.

Montessori, Maria. *The Advanced Montessori Method I*. Vol. 9. Oxford: Clio, 2004. Print. The Clio Montessori Ser.

Montessori, Maria. *The Advanced Montessori Method II*. Vol. 13. Oxford: Clio, 2006. Print. The Clio Montessori Ser.

Montessori, Maria. *The Child, Society, and the World: Unpublished Speeches and Writings*. Vol. 7. Oxford: Clio, 2006. Print. The Clio Montessori Ser.

Montessori, Maria. *Creative Development in the Child*. Ed. Rukmini Ramachandran. Vol. 1. Chennai: Kalakshetra, 2007. Print.

Montessori, Maria. *To Educate the Human Potential*. Vol. 6. Oxford: Clio, 2003. Print. The Clio Montessori Ser.

Newberry, Clare T. *Marshmallow*. New York: HarperCollins Publishers, 1990. Print.

Rey, H.A. *Curious George: 75th Anniversary Edition*. New York: Houghton Mifflin Harcourt Publishing Company, 2016. Print.

Sewell, Anna. *Black Beauty*. New York: HarperCollins Publishers, 1998. Print.

Sulurayok, Matilda. *Kamik's First Sled*. Toronto: Inhabit Media, 2015. Print.

Potter, Beatrix. *The Tale of Peter Rabbit*. New York: Viking Penguin Inc., 1989. Print.

Uluadluak, Donald. *Kamik: An Inuit Puppy Story*. Toronto: Inhabit Media, 2013. Print.

White, E.B. *Charlotte's Web*. New York: HarperCollins Publishers, 1980. Print.

EARLY TEXTILE EDUCATION VIA THE MONTESSORI METHOD

Abstract

Is textile education appropriate for three-and-a-half year old children? Absolutely! This paper explores textile education as presented to young children in a mixed-age, Montessori Primary prepared environment for three through six year old students utilizing universal, child-centered practices which can be applied in other educational settings including the home. Starting at approximately three-and-a-half years of age, children learn how to match or "pair" swatches of various natural fibers by touch in the "Fabric Boxes." Hands-on experience with the contents of the Fabric Boxes acts as both a precursor and a catalyst to more advanced textile studies including fabric identification and pattern recognition as well as lessons pertaining to textile processing, geographical context, and general textile history. Textile vocabulary, specifically the names of various types and weaves of fabrics, is introduced using the enjoyable "Three Period Lesson" technique for effective short and long-term memory retention. Three Period Lessons are followed by "Extensions of the Second Period" and "Extensions of the Third Period" to further reinforce and solidify learned vocabulary. Older students who have attained literacy draw upon their prior textile knowledge in order to participate in relevant reading exercises which may include labeling familiar swatches with provided typed cards. Lessons related to the manufacture of various textiles, cultural geography, and textile history are integrated seamlessly into Montessori's holistic curriculum. The progression of textile studies in the Montessori Primary classroom from straightforward individual presentations with the Fabric Boxes to open-ended advanced literacy and research activities is described in detail to expand reader knowledge and assist implementation.

Introduction

A formal introduction to textile education can begin sooner than you might think. In an authentic Montessori Primary classroom, or "Casa," for three through six year old children, students as young as three-and-a-half are introduced to "Fabric Boxes" as an essential component of their sensorial education. Before describing the contents and objectives of the Fabric Boxes and their related developmental exercises, basic knowledge about the Montessori Method of education is crucial.

A Brief Overview of the Montessori Method

The Montessori Method of education, developed by Dr. Maria Montessori in 1907, is a child-centered educational philosophy which emphasizes student freedom of activity within a developmentally appropriate prepared environment. For optimal results, a cognitively appropriate mixed-age group of children, a complete set of scientific educational materials, a trained Montessori teacher, and a minimum three hour work period are required. In a "Primary prepared environment" or "Casa" for children approximately three though six years of age, students are exposed to a holistic, integrated curriculum which consists of four main subject areas: Practical Life, Sensorial, Language, and Mathematics.[117] Sensorial education, which fosters the development of the five senses and their attributes,[118] includes textile education as a vital component of tactile refinement.[119] Young children are naturally attracted to textile education due to the instinctive and intense proclivities of the age group known to

---

[117] Montessori, Maria. *Dr. Montessori's Own Handbook*. Mineola, NY: Dover Publications, Inc., 2005. Print. Pages 18-20.

[118] Ibid. Pages 30-87.

[119] Montessori, Maria. *Creative Development in the Child: The Montessori Approach*. Ed. Rukmini Ramachandran. Vol. 1. Chennai: Kalakshetra, 2007. Print. Pages 146-166.

Montessori practitioners as "sensitive periods." The four sensitive periods recognized by trained Montessori practitioners, or "Montessorians," are order, movement, refinement of sensory perception, and language. Although humans have a need for order, movement, sensory stimulus, and language throughout the lifespan, the desire to perfect these traits is most intense during early childhood.[120] [121] The desire to perfect order, movement, and sensorial awareness is typically most powerful before four-and-a-half years of age.[122] Keen sensitivity toward language development generally continues through the age of six.[123] Since all sensitive periods are most intense before a child's elementary years,[124] [125] it is essential that students begin to develop awareness of textiles early in life when the ability to do so is most effortless.[126] All activities in the Casa, including textile awareness, are presented holistically and are designed to grow with the student from early childhood to elementary school followed by adolescence and ultimately adulthood.[127] [128] If textile education is presented in a

---

[120] Montessori, Maria. *The Discovery of the Child*. Trans. Mary A. Johnstone. Chennai: Kalakshetra, 2006. Print. Pages 107-138.

[121] Montessori, Maria. *The Absorbent Mind*. Trans. Claude A. Claremont. Vol. 1. Oxford: Clio, 2004. Print. The Clio Montessori Ser. Pages 98-124, 156-162.

[122] Montessori, Maria. *The Discovery of the Child*. Trans. Mary A. Johnstone. Chennai: Kalakshetra, 2006. Print. Pages 244-245.

[123] Montessori, Maria. *The Absorbent Mind*. Trans. Claude A. Claremont. Vol. 1. Oxford: Clio, 2004. Print. The Clio Montessori Ser. Pages 98-124, 156-162.

[124] Montessori, Maria. *The Discovery of the Child*. Trans. Mary A. Johnstone. Chennai: Kalakshetra, 2006. Print. Pages 107-138.

[125] Montessori, Maria. *The Absorbent Mind*. Trans. Claude A. Claremont. Vol. 1. Oxford: Clio, 2004. Print. The Clio Montessori Ser. Pages 98-124, 156-162.

[126] Montessori, Maria. *Creative Development in the Child: The Montessori Approach*. Ed. Rukmini Ramachandran. Vol. 1. Chennai: Kalakshetra, 2007. Print. Pages 206-236.

[127] Montessori, Maria. *The Absorbent Mind*. Trans. Claude A. Claremont. Vol. 1. Oxford: Clio, 2004. Print. The Clio Montessori Ser. Pages 156-174.

[128] Montessori, Maria. *To Educate the Human Potential*. Vol. 6. Oxford: Clio, 2003. Print. The Clio Montessori Ser. Pages 1-11.

hands-on manner at the developmentally appropriate time, generally around three-and-a-half years of age, students receive a solid foundation for future textile work presented in later years.[129]

Prerequisites to Textile Education in the Montessori Casa

Although basic textile education is an integral component of the Montessori Casa, work with fabrics does not typically begin on the first day of school. Before a student can receive any formal lessons with the Fabric Boxes or their related activities, a number of prerequisite skills are required for success. Basic self-control must be established before the child can be entrusted to use textile materials properly. In the Primary classroom, self-control is most often developed through independent work with freely chosen Practical Life, or life skills, exercises.[130] Practical Life activities such as "Carrying a Tray," "Opening and Closing Containers," and "Hand Washing" foster gross and fine motor coordination skills that must be mastered prior to handling delicate fabric swatches. These life skill activities also promote hygiene, positive social skills,[131] and the ability to follow directions in further preparation for formal textile education and other endeavors.[132] In addition to demonstrating good executive function, students must be able to match basic items independently as a vital prerequisite to Fabric Box lessons. The ability to match or "pair" two loose items within a larger set usually begins with the "Thermic Bottles" lesson. In

---

[129] Da Prato, Mary. *My First Montessori Book of Patterns*. United States: CreateSpace Independent Publishing Platform, 2014. Print.

[130] Montessori, Maria. *Creative Development in the Child: The Montessori Approach*. Ed. Rukmini Ramachandran. Vol. 1. Chennai: Kalakshetra, 2007. Print. Pages 182-183.

[131] Montessori, Maria. *The Discovery of the Child*. Trans. Mary A. Johnstone. Chennai: Kalakshetra, 2006. Print. Pages 86-88.

[132] Montessori, Maria. *Creative Development in the Child: The Montessori Approach*. Ed. Rukmini Ramachandran. Vol. 1. Chennai: Kalakshetra, 2007. Print. Pages 175-183.

this simple matching activity, the Montessori teacher or "guide" prepares child-sized bottles which allow an individual student to match cold, cool, warm, and hot temperatures by touch. (For safety, an adult always controls the temperature of the bottles prior to student use.) While seemingly unrelated to work with textiles, the ability to pair Thermic Bottles fosters learning readiness for matching fabrics by texture, which is the first formal textile lesson a student typically receives in the Casa.

Following mastery of all the aforementioned prerequisites, a student is generally ready for the first introduction to textile education around three-and-a-half years of age. This age is a general guideline as lessons are taught or "presented" in the Casa when an individual student displays interest and readiness rather than according to a predetermined rubric.

Introduction to Textile Education with the Fabric Boxes

A child's first formal introduction to the world of textiles begins with a one-on-one lesson from the teacher or guide using the first of the Casa's two Fabric Boxes. The first Fabric Box in the Primary prepared environment is known as "Fabric Box 1." There is no official Fabric Box 1 that a Montessori guide must purchase for the classroom, so each Casa may have its own unique box for storing fabric swatches chosen and assembled. The contents of Fabric Box 1 are also the guide's responsibility, although certain guidelines must be followed. Fabric Box 1 should be an attractive, child-sized square or rectangular container that can hold five or six pairs of fabric swatches. A box with a lid is preferred for organizational and aesthetic purposes. Each fabric swatch in Fabric Box 1 should be the same size for matching by touch. Pairs of swatches in the Casa are always made of natural materials such as cotton, denim, hemp, linen, and silk. As a hybrid fabric made of natural cellulose fibers,[133] rayon swatches are also appropriate for

Fabric Box 1. Swatches of leather and chamois[134] may also be included. To maintain student interest, and to maximize exposure to a variety of fabric types, the guide occasionally exchanges fabric swatches in Fabric Box 1 for different fabrics. Keep in mind that specialty weaves such as brocade, silk charmeuse, and tapestry are placed in Fabric Box 2, which is introduced following mastery of Fabric Box 1.

When an individual student is ready for the first Fabric Box lesson, the guide invites the child to attend a presentation. It is important that the child does not feel compelled to attend the Fabric Box 1 presentation as forcing participation may instill a reluctance to work with textiles in the future.[135] Montessori education honors the innate curiosity of children by presenting lessons which best suit an individual student's needs and interests at a given time. If a child is not currently interested in working with fabric swatches, the lesson is put away for another time and reintroduced when the student shows interest.

Once the student accepts the guide's invitation to receive a lesson, Fabric Box 1 is placed on a child-sized work table. Before touching any of the swatches, the guide and student wash their hands to avoid soiling any of the fabrics with the hands' natural oils. A child who has mastered the prerequisite Practical Life exercise "Hand Washing" is ready to perform this task with little effort. After the guide and child wash their hands, the guide may invite the student to perform a task known as "Sensitizing

---

[133] Salusso, Carol J. "Rayon" *Encyclopedia of Clothing and Fashion.* 3rd ed. Detroit: Charles Scribner's Sons, 2005.

[134] Angus, Emily, Macushla Baudis, and Philippa Woodcock. *The Fashion Encyclopedia: A Visual Resource for Terms, Techniques, and Styles.* 1st ed. Hauppauge, NY: Barron's Educational Series, Inc., 2015. Print. Pages 234, 280-285.

[135] Montessori, Maria. *Creative Development in the Child: The Montessori Approach.* Ed. Rukmini Ramachandran. Vol. 1. Chennai: Kalakshetra, 2007. Print. Pages 152-154.

Fingertips." An optional preliminary exercise, Sensitizing Fingertips refers to the act of submerging the fingertips in warm water followed by briskly rubbing them dry with a clean terry towel. This series of actions is designed to temporarily increase the sensitivity of the child's fingertips in order to heighten the upcoming tactile experience with the swatches in Fabric Box 1.

Upon returning to the child-sized work table, the guide opens Fabric Box 1 and demonstrates the proper technique for feeling each fabric swatch. In the Casa, a swatch is handled by rubbing it between both palms in order to experience the texture of the fabric across a large surface area, including the fingertips which may have been previously sensitized. The guide typically performs this action silently so the child can watch the proper movements without any unnecessary distractions. Following the guide's demonstration, the child is invited to take a turn feeling the fabric swatch as modeled. The name of the textile the child is holding is not introduced at this time to prevent distracting the student from the present tactile experience of feeling the fabric between the palms of the hands. This practice of allowing the child to fully experience the nature and composition of a given material before learning its accompanying vocabulary is known in Montessori education as "experience precedes language." By allowing the child to feel various swatches before introducing vocabulary, the guide helps create a foundation for learning. By completing hands-on work without the distraction of unfamiliar vocabulary, the student will be prepared to truly understand and retain the proper vocabulary when it is finally presented at a later time.[136]

After the child finishes feeling the first fabric swatch in Fabric Box 1, the guide sets it aside on the right-hand side of the table, and then removes the second swatch from the box. Like the first swatch, the guide demonstrates how to feel the second swatch

---

[136] Montessori, Maria. *Dr. Montessori's Own Handbook*. Mineola, NY: Dover Publications, Inc., 2005. Print. Pages 80-84.

between the palms of the hands and then gives the child a turn. This process is repeated with each swatch in the box until the first duplicate swatch is found. When the duplicate fabric swatches, designed for pairing, are discovered at the bottom of Fabric Box 1, the guide explains to the child that they are the same as the swatches they just felt.

It is now time to begin matching fabric swatches by touch. To do this, the guide organizes the first set of fabric swatches on the right-hand side of the table into a column with space between each swatch. The second set of swatches is placed in a column with space between each swatch on the left-hand side of the table across from the first set. When organizing the swatches, the guide is careful not to place identical swatches across from one another as this would defeat the purpose of the game, which is to match swatches that have been mixed up. Once the swatches are ready to use, the guide puts on a blindfold and matches the pairs of swatches by touch to model gameplay. After pairing all the swatches, the guide removes the blindfold to see if everything is matched correctly. It is now the child's turn. The guide disassembles the paired swatches and reorganizes them into two columns on opposite sides of the table. When everything is in place, the child may begin pairing fabric swatches as demonstrated by the guide. For hygiene, the child will either have a personal blindfold or will place a clean piece of facial tissue between the eyes and a communal blindfold. All blindfolds in the Casa are washed frequently for cleanliness.[137]

When the child finishes pairing fabric swatches in Fabric Box 1, the student may repeat the activity as many times as desired. Any child who has had a lesson for Fabric Box 1 may select the activity whenever it is available on the shelf during the uninterrupted three hour work period. It is not uncommon for a

---

[137] Da Prato, Mary. *My First Montessori Book of Patterns*. United States: CreateSpace Independent Publishing Platform, 2014. Print.

young child, particularly under four-and-a-half years of age, to voluntarily repeat the same activity forty or more times in succession in order to master an activity.[138] Repetition of educational exercises in this manner is a vital developmental process for young children and generally not a cause for concern.[139]

Textile Vocabulary Presentations for Fabric Box 1

Following an individual student's success pairing swatches in Fabric Box 1, the guide prepares a number of follow-up activities to further the child's textile education. The first of these lessons focuses upon vocabulary, specifically, learning the names of the fabrics the child has been pairing in Fabric Box 1. Vocabulary is most frequently introduced using the effective and enjoyable "Three Period Lesson" technique of "Naming," "Recognition," and "Remembering," which is introduced as a game. Everything in the Casa has a name, and children six years of age and younger can learn any vocabulary, including names of textiles, if it is introduced in an age-appropriate manner.[140] Due to young children's intense interest in language acquisition, the guide is entrusted to introduce as much relevant technical vocabulary as possible.[141]

To introduce the names of various fabrics, the guide removes three contrasting fabric swatches from Fabric Box 1 such as cotton, linen, and wool. The guide places the three chosen swatches

---

[138] Montessori, Maria. *The Secret of Childhood*. Trans. Barbara B. Carter. Hyderabad: Orient Longman, 2006. Print. Pages 124-127.

[139] Montessori, Maria. *Creative Development in the Child: The Montessori Approach*. Ed. Rukmini Ramachandran. Vol. 1. Chennai: Kalakshetra, 2007. Print. Pages 54-59.

[140] Montessori, Maria. *The Absorbent Mind*. Trans. Claude A. Claremont. Vol. 1. Oxford: Clio, 2004. Print. The Clio Montessori Ser. Pages 158-165.

[141] Montessori, Maria. *Creative Development in the Child: The Montessori Approach*. Ed. Rukmini Ramachandran. Vol. 1. Chennai: Kalakshetra, 2007. Print. Pages 214-217.

horizontally on a child-sized work table or rug with space between each swatch and invites the child to play a game. Once the child accepts the guide's invitation, the Three Period Lesson begins.

During "Naming," the guide points to each fabric swatch from left to right in turn and clearly states the name of each as in, "This is 'cotton.' This is 'linen.' This is 'wool.'" Once each vocabulary term is introduced in this manner, the "Naming" period of the Three Period Lesson is complete. No further commentary is provided to prevent overwhelming or confusing the child.

During "Recognition," the longest stage of the Three Period Lesson, the guide reinforces the introduced vocabulary by playing a simple game with the fabric swatches. To play, the guide gives one command at a time which uses the presented vocabulary as in, "Hand me the 'linen,'" "Point to the 'cotton,'" or "Put the 'wool' here." To encourage meaningful interaction with the fabric swatches, tactile commands such as, "Touch the 'cotton'" or "Feel the 'linen'" may also be given. If the child misidentifies a swatch, the guide states the correct answer as in, "This is 'linen.' Now point to 'cotton.'" The "Recognition" phase of the Three Period Lesson continues until the child is confident with the vocabulary or loses interest.

The final stage of the Three Period Lesson, "Remembering," is the period in which the child is asked to recall the presented vocabulary from memory. During this stage of the activity, the guide points to one of the swatches and asks, "What is this?" Following correct identification of the swatch, the guide points to another swatch and asks the same question. Finally, the guide points to the third swatch and asks the child to identify it. If the child misidentifies any of the swatches, or is unable to think of the answer, the guide states the correct answer as in, "This is 'linen.'" Unfamiliar vocabulary is reviewed at a later time if necessary. Once the child correctly identifies each of the three fabric swatches by name, the guide reinforces the student's newfound knowledge and encourages additional activity by saying something like, "You learned 'cotton,' 'linen,' and 'wool.' Would you like to learn three more fabrics?" If the child expresses interest in learning more, the guide puts the swatches away and chooses three new swatches such as hemp, rayon, and denim. The Three Period Lesson is then presented with those three swatches. After the second Three Period Lesson for fabric names is complete, the guide thanks the child for playing, and asks what the student would like to do next. Typically, only three to six new vocabulary words per category are introduced per day to avoid overwhelming the child and to give adequate time to process new information.

Keep in mind that Three Period Lessons are presented as enjoyable games and are not forced. If a child loses interest in the middle of a Three Period Lesson, the guide ends the activity for the day by thanking the child for playing and then asking what the student would like to do next. Learning the names of textiles can and should be a pleasant educational experience. The guide is careful to keep such lessons fun by maintaining a flexible schedule and atmosphere.[142]

Reinforcement of Short and Long-Term Textile Memory

Shortly after a successful Three Period Lesson for textile vocabulary, the guide introduces activities to help reinforce the child's newfound knowledge. The most common of these activities are known as the "Three Period Review," "Extensions of the Second Period," and "Extensions of the Third Period." The Three Period Review is designed to review and reinforce recently learned vocabulary. The objectives of Extensions of the Second Period and Extensions of the Third Period are 1) enrichment and reinforcement of vocabulary, 2) classification of items and concepts in the surrounding environment to assist the sensitive period for order, 3) development of self-confidence with language

---

[142] Da Prato, Mary. *My First Montessori Book of Patterns*. United States: CreateSpace Independent Publishing Platform, 2014. Print.

in preparation for successful literacy and creative writing (which may include researching and writing about textiles in later years if the child so chooses), and 4) moving from general classifications to more specific classifications in preparation for elementary level studies (e.g. a general classification could be "fabrics" while a specific classification could be "fabrics which originate from plants"). Three Period Reviews, Extensions of the Second Period, and Extensions of the Third Period in relation to textile education are described in the following paragraphs.

Three Period Review of Textile Vocabulary

To review recently introduced textile vocabulary, the guide may place fabric swatches in a pile and ask the child to identify each one from memory. Swatches the child knows are placed in one stack while unfamiliar or challenging swatches are placed in another stack. When all fabric swatches have been sorted, the stack of familiar swatches is set aside. Three unfamiliar or challenging swatches from the unfamiliar stack are brought to the center of the table and laid out with space between each swatch. The guide then presents a typical Three Period Lesson using the three stages of "Naming," "Recognition," and "Remembering." Following the Three Period Lesson, the learned swatches are put in the familiar stack. The child is then invited to learn three more fabric names or conclude the activity. If the child chooses to learn three more fabric names, the guide chooses three unfamiliar fabric swatches and gives another Three Period Lesson. At the end of the lesson, all fabric swatches are returned to their box for another day. The child is then free to pursue other work.[143]

---

[143] Ibid.

Extensions of the Second Period to Review Textile Vocabulary

Often called the "Bring Me Game," Extensions of the Second Period strengthens students' short and long-term memories of previously introduced vocabulary in a particular chosen topic such as "Textile Identification." Extensions of the Second Period can be played with an individual child but is often suited to small groups of approximately two to five students who have had prior experience with the same vocabulary. When possible, groups include students of various ages so older children can model the activity for their younger peers. Younger students who have not yet learned textile vocabulary are welcome to observe. At the guide's discretion, young students who lack textile knowledge may become the partner of an older student during the activity to promote textile awareness and a positive attitude toward receiving formal textile lessons in the future.

To play Extensions of the Second Period with the names of various textiles, the guide places all the fabric swatches for the activity on a child-sized table a distance from where the exercise will be presented. The guide then invites one available student at a time to play a game until the group is full. Student players are then gathered at a work rug or stand in a line in front of the teacher's chair. The guide gives a specific command to one child in the group. If possible, the guide gives the most experienced child in the group the first turn to model gameplay. The older and more experienced the child is, the more complex the command can be. An example of a simple command for a younger player may be, "Bring me a cotton swatch, (Child's Name)." In contrast, a more complex command for an older player may be, "Bring me a blue striped fabric swatch made of cotton, (Child's Name)." Note how the child's name is always stated after the command to encourage all students in the group to listen.

When the child returns with the swatch, the guide confirms what the child has brought. If it is the correct swatch, the guide says, "You brought me the cotton swatch! Now you can take the swatch back." Note how the guide says the child "can" take the swatch back instead of the child "may" take the swatch back. This wording emphasizes the child's abilities as opposed to granting permission for a task the student is ready to perform independently.

If the child has brought the incorrect swatch, the guide says something like, "Oh! You brought me the rayon swatch. Now bring me the cotton swatch." If the child continues to struggle, the guide may suggest that the student choose a friend to help locate the correct swatch. When such interventions are necessary, the guide is always careful to be kind, considerate, and supportive of a struggling child rather than critical.

While one child in the group is retrieving a requested fabric swatch, the other children in the group may become restless. To combat boredom and the negative behaviors that might arise from it, the guide keeps the waiting children productively occupied by discussing the current game topic as in, "We certainly have a lot of fabric swatches in our classroom! Which one was (Child's Name) supposed to find? That's right! He is looking for cotton. How does cotton feel? Is it soft or rough?" These types of filler conversations not only help keep students engaged while waiting their turn but assist with language development in regard to textiles.

Extensions of the Second Period continues until each child in the group has had at least one turn. The guide then dismisses one student at a time to find other work. Fabric swatches are returned to their appropriate box and returned to the shelf. Once the Fabric Box is returned to the shelf, any child who has received a lesson from the guide may choose to pair swatches as an independent activity.

Extensions of the Third Period to Solidify Textile Vocabulary

Extensions of the Third Period is an abstract exercise that draws upon students' long-term memories of textile vocabulary introduced during Three Period Lessons and reviewed during Three Period Reviews as well as Extensions of the Second Period. Unlike prior vocabulary activities, Extensions of the Third Period uses no visual aids and relies completely upon memory. Extensions of the Third Period can be played with an individual child but is often better suited to a small group of approximately three to seven students.

To begin Extensions of the Third Period, the guide invites one child at a time to play a game until the group is full. If possible, a mixed-age group is invited to model gameplay as well as highlight various levels of textile knowledge. The group typically gathers at a rug. Once the group is settled, the guide introduces the topic by saying something like, "Let's name all the types of fabric we can think of- like cotton!" The children are then free to call out any fabric names they can think of as soon as they come to mind. Students do not need to raise their hands during this activity as doing so would disrupt the flow of the game. If the game slows down, the guide may suggest another fabric name, but the majority of the textile vocabulary is supplied by the children. The game continues until the children run out of fabric names, or lose interest in the activity. To conclude, the guide thanks the children for playing and then dismisses the students one at a time to find other work.

Related Textile Activities for Fabric Box 1

Related activities in the Casa for any given topic are generally open-ended and presented based upon the guide's observations of student needs, interests, and cognitive readiness. Following are some possible examples of how a Montessori guide may heighten a student's awareness of textiles in both the Casa and wider world.[144]

Sewing Projects

Children in the Casa begin to receive hand sewing lessons starting around four to four-and-a-half years of age, although the age of the initial presentation is based upon observed readiness. Following mastery of the presentation "Sewing a Button," the student is introduced to increasingly complex hand sewing exercises such as embroidery and making a miniature pillow. When a child has had ample experience with basic sewing activities, the guide may reintroduce familiar fabrics originally presented in Fabric Box 1 for additional sewing projects in order to promote further tactile experience.

Picture Cards for Pattern Recognition

Although not an official presentation in the Casa, pattern recognition is one of many activities the guide is at liberty to create based upon observed need and interest. If the guide chooses to formally introduce the names of patterns such as "stripes," "herringbone," and "checks," these features may be pointed out directly on fabric swatches present in Fabric Box 1. Alternatively, "Picture Cards" may be created to isolate each pattern.

Picture Cards, which resemble unlabeled flashcards, are used in the Casa to introduce vocabulary when it is impractical or impossible to provide the actual object each card represents. Up to ten Picture Cards of the same category or classification may be placed in a single deck. Classifications may be general as in "patterns" or specific as in "patterns found in nature" or "patterns found on fabrics." Each Picture Card isolates a clear image of one item to be learned. Picture Cards have no writing, making this pre-literacy activity a guide-directed exercise. Picture Cards and

---

[144] Ibid.

Picture Card Sets are rotated frequently to expose children to a variety of vocabulary.

Like physical objects in the environment, Picture Card vocabulary is presented using the typical Three Period Lesson technique. The guide isolates three unfamiliar cards with contrasting images such as "stripes," "herringbone," and "checks" and then begins the Three Period Lesson cycle of "Naming," "Remembering," and "Recognition."[145] Short and long-term memory of Picture Card vocabulary that has been introduced using the Three Period Lesson technique is then reinforced and solidified using Three Period Reviews, Extensions of the Second Period, and Extensions of the Third Period.

Textile Labels and Pattern Three Part Cards

Literate students who are confident with the names of various fabrics may be invited to label familiar fabrics with typed cards provided by the guide. Typed labels in the Casa isolate one vocabulary word per card such as "rayon." For clarity and visibility, cards are usually typed using 42 point Century Gothic lowercase font. A deck of related labels is usually placed in a card holder on a shelf near the vocabulary that is going to be labeled. Following a brief presentation from the guide, the child is free to label fabric swatches at a child-sized table or rug whenever the activity is available during the uninterrupted three hour work period.

In addition to labels, "Three Part Cards" are provided as an extension to Picture Cards. As the name implies, Three Part Cards consist of three separate parts: unlabeled Picture Cards, Typed Labels, and Control Cards. To demonstrate how to use the Three Part Cards, the guide invites a child to work at a child-sized table or rug. To introduce a set of Three Part Cards for patterns, the

---

[145] Ibid.

guide begins by showing the student the unlabeled Picture Cards, which are identical to the previously introduced Picture Card Set. Unlabeled Picture Cards are neatly laid out on the work surface with space between each card. The corresponding Typed Labels are placed in a stack, face up, at the bottom center of the work space for the child to label one Picture Card at a time. When finished, the child verifies the accuracy of the work by using the Control Cards, which are correctly labeled Picture Cards. After correcting any errors, the child is free to repeat the activity as many times as desired during the work period, or put the activity away for another time.[146]

Reading Classification for Textiles in the Environment

A guide-directed activity known as "Reading Classification: Objects in the Environment" is an excellent opportunity for literate children of various reading levels to practice reading comprehension while simultaneously reinforcing prior textile vocabulary. To begin, the guide invites one to five literate students to play a game. A group of three student players is optimal. Once the students are settled, the guide states the topic of the game, such as "textiles." The guide then writes a word, phrase, or sentence pertaining to textiles on a slip of paper. The length of the written command depends upon each individual student's reading level. If the child is a beginning reader, the guide may simply write the word "silk." For an intermediate reader, the command may instead read, "Find a silk swatch." An advanced reader may be given the complex command, "Quietly take this label and place it beside a rectangular swatch of yellow silk." Regardless of what the slip says, the child to whom the command is directed must take the slip of paper, find an example of silk in the environment, label it, and return to the group. The child does not need to read the label aloud

---

[146] Ibid.

as its placement in the room will determine whether or not the student understood its meaning.

At the end of the game, the guide has one child at a time collect the same number of slips as he has had turns. A child who had two turns, for example, should find and collect two slips. The most inexperienced children are invited to collect slips first so they have greater exposure to more advanced writing commands left by their peers and so they can collect their own simpler slips, if they choose. The slips do not need to be the ones the child placed. At the end of the game, the guide collects the slips the children have retrieved and places them in a special box where literate students may read them independently as an optional work choice. (Slips are discarded at the end of the school day or school week in a recycling bin.) Once the slips have been placed in the box, the students are dismissed one at a time to find other work.

Independent Writing Activities

Students in the Casa are provided with a number of literacy materials including Movable Alphabets, which are cutout letter forms used for building words, in addition to pencils and paper. These materials may be used for original compositions following applicable lessons from the guide. The Montessori guide does not specifically assign writing topics as creative writing endeavors are left to student choice. If a student is unsure what to write about, the guide can make a recommendation, although this is not always necessary. Given this freedom to write, there is no telling what students will ultimately compose, perhaps even a list of favorite fabric swatches! The guide is attentive to student writing in order to encourage individual expression. Based upon this information, the guide can design relevant individualized lesson plans to foster enjoyable educational experiences and lay a foundation for future learning. For some students, this could possibly be the start of appreciation and a lifelong interest in textiles.

Textile Manufacturing, History, and Geography

The Montessori guide presents a variety of information to three through six year old students in a number of age-appropriate ways. In addition to presenting hands-on experiences followed by vocabulary lessons, the guide also exposes her students to simple manufacturing, history, and geography lessons using a variety of activities including "Telling True Stories," "Puzzle Maps," and "Geography Folders." Following are some examples of open-ended activities the guide may present to further student awareness and understanding of textiles in preparation for further studies which continue in the elementary years.

Telling True Stories about Textiles

"Telling True Stories" is an essential language development activity presented daily to all Primary students starting on the first day of school. By telling an age-appropriate true story to a group of students from memory, the Montessori guide models the essential life skills of how to tell a story and how to listen to a story in order to strengthen short and long-term auditory memory and stoke burgeoning imaginations. Topics for Telling True Stories vary considerably in each Montessori classroom based upon the guide's culture and experiences but may include factual stories about the history of various textiles. One such story could be a simple introduction to the history of silk.

To tell an age-appropriate true story about the history of silk, the guide must first do research outside of class. This may involve visiting the library and creating an applicable visual aid such as a laminated poster that illustrates the silk production process from silk worms to a finished garment. The guide may refer to this visual aid during the presentation and temporarily make it available for independent student viewing afterwards. Visual aids, while not required for Telling a True Story, can be a helpful accompaniment to the guide's oral presentation.

When the guide is ready to tell a story about silk to a group of students, she is always mindful of the cognitive level of the current group. Since young children generally live in the present moment,[147] the guide limits the use of specific dates during simple history presentations. Instead of using precise dates, the guide puts the story in a more general historical context by saying something like, "A long time ago, long before you were born, before your parents were born, and even before your grandparents were born..." This introduction generally provides the appropriate level of context when presenting history to a young child.

If a history lesson is cognitively too advanced for young students, the guide may instead tell a story about how a silk worm spins a cocoon and how cocoons are unraveled to make silk, as these processes still occur today. Regardless of whether the guide chooses to explain silk from a modern or historical perspective, Telling True Stories is an activity which should be kept brief in order to accommodate short attention spans. Instead of bombarding students with too much information in a single story, the guide may tell several stories about silk over the course of a few days or weeks depending upon student interest.[148] [149]

Reading Books about Textiles

In addition to Telling True Stories, the Montessori guide can read simple non-fiction picture books about textiles to small groups of interested students, or the whole class simultaneously if

---

[147] Montessori, Maria. *The Child, Society, and the World: Unpublished Speeches and Writings*. Vol. 7. Oxford: Clio, 2006. Print. The Clio Montessori Ser. Pages 4-9.

[148] Da Prato, Mary. *My First Montessori Book of Patterns*. United States: CreateSpace Independent Publishing Platform, 2014. Print.

[149] Da Prato, Mary. *The Peace Table*. The Montessori Mystery Unveiled Series. United States: CreateSpace Independent Publishing Platform, 2015. Print.

the children choose to participate. Narrative works about textile production, such as *The Empress and the Silkworm* by Lily Toy Hong,[150] may also provide an introduction to the history of silk in a manner that is both accessible and enjoyable for young children. Later in the week, additional books related to textiles, a simple history of the Silk Road, and geographical context shown on a globe or map may be introduced as well. Books read by the Montessori guide are typically made available for independent student viewing in the "Reading Corner" for further exposure to textile information. Children who have not yet received a Fabric Box presentation or its related vocabulary activities are welcome to listen to stories and look at picture books independently as a foundation for formal studies when ready.

Geography Presentations as a Means of Fostering Textile Awareness

"Puzzle Maps" and "Geography Folders," two open-ended geography activities in the Casa, provide an excellent introduction to international textile awareness. Knobbed Puzzle Maps give children a hands-on introduction to geography knowledge such as where textile weaves originated while simultaneously fostering the development of spatial relationship skills. In addition to their obvious use as puzzles, Puzzle Maps are used in the Casa as a concrete connection between physical geography and explorations of culture. For example, if a guide is telling a story about the origin and history of silk, the Puzzle Map piece which represents China may be used as a visual aid to help solidify understanding of where the textile originally came from.

Another open-ended geography activity, Geography Folders are filled with pictures of people, places, and things from around the world to expose students to life outside of their culture in a

---

[150] Hong, Lily Toy. *The Empress and the Silkworm*. Morton Grove, IL: Albert Whitman & Company, 1995. Print.

universally appealing, respectful manner. For organizational purposes, each Geography Folder represents one continent. Within each Geography Folder are a number of photographs which generally depict people going about their daily lives, which may include wearing regional dress or doing traditional handicrafts such as weaving. Pictures in the Geography Folders, which are rotated occasionally to maintain interest and maximize exposure to other cultures, may be used in a number of ways in the Casa. For example, the guide may include photographs of silk worms and the silk production process in the Geography Folder of Asia. Photographs of people wearing traditional or contemporary silk garments for special occasions are another possibility. Regardless of the photographs the guide chooses, she is careful to present any information in a respectful, factual, and unbiased manner to prevent subconsciously instilling prejudice in young impressionable children.

While suitable as a visual aid for group activities, Geography Folder pictures are also appropriate for individual presentations such as "Facilitated Conversations." During a Facilitated Conversation with the Geography Folders, the guide invites a child to look at a particular photograph, such as a picture of a person weaving. Together, the guide and student discuss their observations of the photograph. Throughout the discussion, the guide casually interjects any relevant information about the scene depicted. For example, the guide may point out the loom and a few of its parts such as the treadles, heddles, warp, and weft. This vocabulary may be reinforced during a formal Three Period Lesson at a later time. The guide may also describe the general weaving process. Exactly how much information the guide conveys depends upon the child's cognitive abilities and level of interest. When the Facilitated Conversation comes to a close, the guide returns to other tasks. The child is then free to look at Geography Folder pictures independently or with a friend who has received a lesson.[151]

Introduction to Specialty Fabric Weaves with Fabric Box 2

Like Fabric Box 1, Fabric Box 2 is filled with five or six pairs of fabric swatches for children to match by touch. Fabric Box 2 showcases a variety of specialty fabric weaves such as brocade, corduroy, silk charmeuse, tapestry, and tulle for the child's further textile knowledge and exploration. Since students have had ample experience with textiles from Fabric Box 1, the presentation of Fabric Box 2 is deliberately minimal. When the child exhausts the possibilities of Fabric Box 1, the guide shows the child Fabric Box 2 and says it is used in the same manner as Fabric Box 1. This limited but clear information is typically enough for the child to pair swatches in Fabric Box 2 successfully. Related follow-up activities presented for Fabric Box 1, including vocabulary, history, and geography, are also introduced with the swatches showcased in Fabric Box 2.[152]

Textile Research for Older Students

Students in the Casa who are about six years of age will soon transition to elementary school, possibly to a Montessori Elementary program. To assist with this transition, the guide helps her older students learn how to seek information from credible sources. A dictionary or encyclopedia may be made available to older students in the Casa for this purpose. Children in the Casa are free to research various topics of interest, although the actual act of doing research is not required until the elementary years. Older students who are inspired to learn more about textiles outside of the guide's presentations are permitted and encouraged to study the

---

[151] Da Prato, Mary. *The Peace Table*. The Montessori Mystery Unveiled Series. United States: CreateSpace Independent Publishing Platform, 2015. Print. Pages 92-98.

[152] Da Prato, Mary. *My First Montessori Book of Patterns*. United States: CreateSpace Independent Publishing Platform, 2014. Print.

topic independently or with a peer. The guide assists with the process of student-directed research as needed. Keep in mind that performing any kind of research requires a certain level of cognitive maturity that most students will not attain until the end of their Primary years or the beginning of their Montessori Elementary years.[153] For this reason, research projects are not an official component of the Primary prepared environment. Nonetheless, the guide should be prepared to assist older students who are eager and ready for this level of challenge.

Textile Education in Montessori Elementary and Beyond

Textile education starting at approximately three-and-a-half years of age in the Montessori Primary prepared environment helps lay a solid foundation for further textile education during the Montessori Elementary curriculum for six through twelve year old students. When various fabrics and their accompanying vocabulary are introduced during a child's sensitive periods for order, movement, sensory perception, and language, the student comes to elementary school ready for more advanced related work.[154] Textile activities in the Montessori Elementary classroom may include sewing,[155] quilting,[156] weaving,[157] knitting, and costume

---

[153] Montessori, Maria. *From Childhood to Adolescence Including "Erdkinder" and the Functions of the University*. Vol. 12. Amsterdam: Montessori-Pierson Publishing Company, 2007. Print. The Montessori Ser. Pages 5, 17-23.

[154] Montessori, Maria. *To Educate the Human Potential*. Vol. 6. Oxford: Clio, 2003. Print. The Clio Montessori Ser. Pages 1-11.

[155] Teachers and Students of Mountain Laurel Montessori School. "Work of the Hand Through the Curriculum and Across the Planes of Development: A Compilation of Creative Ideas." Ed. David Kahn. The NAMTA Journal 38.2 (2013): 113. Print.

[156] Nixon, Monica. "Quilt-Making in the Elementary Class." Ed. David Kahn. *The NAMTA Journal* 38.2 (2013): 121–124. Print.

[157] "Elementary." *Butler Montessori*. Butler Montessori, 2016. Web. 27 Dec. 2016. https://butlerschool.org/learning-doing/elementary/.

design.[158] Montessori Elementary students also use timelines to study the history of various topics which may include the history of textiles. Geography, initially introduced in the Primary prepared environment, continues to be an important aspect of the Montessori curriculum during the elementary years. Topics such as international imports and exports of various goods in both the past and present are also covered. Textiles can be holistically integrated into these larger topics of discussion for students who are interested.

When possible, graduating Montessori Elementary students may continue their studies during adolescence in a program known as "Erdkinder." Erdkinder, German for "earth children,"[159] focuses on preparing students twelve through fifteen or twelve through eighteen years of age to become fully functional members of society upon reaching adulthood.[160] Adolescents in a Montessori Erdkinder program learn how to become increasingly self-sufficient in their daily lives and often begin to dabble in trades of interest under experienced adult guidance. Like their younger counterparts, Montessori Erdkinder students continue to study both academic and creative subjects in a holistic fashion that appeals to adolescent interests and sensibilities. Adolescents also typically develop an interest in how both machines and social systems work. A desire to engage in commercial activity becomes apparent as well.[161] In order to fulfill these adolescent needs and interests, the Erdkinder program provides an environment which allows students

[158] Stephenson, Susan Mayclin. *Child of the World: Montessori, Global Education for Age 3-12+*. Arcata, CA: Michael Olaf Montessori Company, 2013. Print. Page 101.

[159] Lillard, Paula Polk. *Montessori Today*. New York: Schocken Books, 1996. Print. Page 159.

[160] Montessori, Maria. *From Childhood to Adolescence Including "Erdkinder" and the Functions of the University*. Vol. 12. Amsterdam: Montessori-Pierson Publishing Company, 2007. Print. The Montessori Ser. Page 60.

[161] Ibid. Pages 59-70.

to learn how specific technologies function (such as how an automatic weaving loom or industrial sewing machine work) as well as how humans have traded technologies, goods, and ideas throughout history in order to meet their physical, intellectual, and emotional requirements.[162] [163] These lessons may culminate in the adolescent student running a stand at a farmer's market or apprenticing in the textile or other industries as part of the holistic curriculum.[164] At this time, the student may sell his original creations to customers in the local community. If the student finds selling arts and crafts both emotionally and financially rewarding, the interest may continue into a career.[165]

Conclusion

Will the three-and-a-half year old child who becomes immersed in the Fabric Boxes become the next great textile expert or fashion designer? Who knows? All we can do is make textile education accessible from an early age by presenting cognitively appropriate experiences in a loving manner. One day, many years from now, a professor of textiles or a famous fashion designer may say during an interview, "It all started when I was about three years old."

---

[162] Lillard, Paula Polk. *Montessori Today*. New York: Schocken Books, 1996. Print. Page 159.

[163] Bell, Aurora, Renee Ergazos, Annie Frazer, and Renee Pendleton, Eds. *The Whole-School Montessori Handbook for Teachers and Administrators: The Evolution of a Montessori High School.* Supplement 2013–2015 ed. Burton, OH: North American Montessori Teachers' Association, 2015. Print. Pages 155-182. http://www.montessori-namta.org/Print-Publications/School-Operations-and-Administration/Supplement-2013-2015.

[164] Stephenson, Susan Mayclin. *Child of the World: Montessori, Global Education for Age 3-12+*. Arcata, CA: Michael Olaf Montessori Company, 2013. Print. Pages 127-135.

[165] Ibid. Pages 133-135.

References

Angus, Emily, Macushla Baudis, and Philippa Woodcock. *The Fashion Encyclopedia: A Visual Resource for Terms, Techniques, and Styles*. 1st ed. Hauppauge, NY: Barron's Educational Series, Inc., 2015. Print.

Bell, Aurora, Renee Ergazos, Annie Frazer, and Renee Pendleton, Eds. *The Whole-School Montessori Handbook for Teachers and Administrators: The Evolution of a Montessori High School*. Supplement 2013–2015 ed. Burton, OH: North American Montessori Teachers' Association, 2015. Print. http://www.montessori-namta.org/Print-Publications/School-Operations-and-Administration/Supplement-2013-2015.

"Elementary." *Butler Montessori*. Butler Montessori, 2016. Web. 27 Dec. 2016. https://butlerschool.org/learning-doing/elementary/.

Da Prato, Mary. *My First Montessori Book of Patterns*. United States: CreateSpace Independent Publishing Platform, 2014. Print.

Da Prato, Mary. *The Peace Table*. The Montessori Mystery Unveiled Series. United States: CreateSpace Independent Publishing Platform, 2015. Print.

Hong, Lily Toy. *The Empress and the Silkworm*. Morton Grove, IL: Albert Whitman & Company, 1995. Print.

Lillard, Paula Polk. *Montessori Today*. New York: Schocken Books, 1996. Print.

Montessori, Maria. *The Absorbent Mind*. Trans. Claude A. Claremont. Vol. 1. Oxford: Clio, 2004. Print. The Clio Montessori Ser.

Montessori, Maria. *The Child, Society, and the World: Unpublished Speeches and Writings*. Vol. 7. Oxford: Clio, 2006. Print. The Clio Montessori Ser.

Montessori, Maria. *Creative Development in the Child: The Montessori Approach*. Ed. Rukmini Ramachandran. Vol. 1. Chennai: Kalakshetra, 2007. Print.

Montessori, Maria. *The Discovery of the Child*. Trans. Mary A. Johnstone. Chennai: Kalakshetra, 2006. Print.

Montessori, Maria. *Dr. Montessori's Own Handbook*. Mineola, NY: Dover Publications, Inc., 2005. Print.

Montessori, Maria. *From Childhood to Adolescence Including "Erdkinder" and the Functions of the University*. Vol. 12. Amsterdam: Montessori-Pierson Publishing Company, 2007. Print. The Montessori Ser.

Montessori, Maria. *The Secret of Childhood*. Trans. Barbara B. Carter. Hyderabad: Orient Longman, 2006. Print.

Montessori, Maria. *To Educate the Human Potential*. Vol. 6. Oxford: Clio, 2003. Print. The Clio Montessori Ser.

Nixon, Monica. "Quilt-Making in the Elementary Class." Ed. David Kahn. *The NAMTA Journal* 38.2 (2013): 120–124. Print.

Salusso, Carol J. "Rayon" *Encyclopedia of Clothing and Fashion*. 3rd ed. Detroit: Charles Scribner's Sons, 2005.

Stephenson, Susan Mayclin. *Child of the World: Montessori, Global Education for Age 3-12+*. Arcata, CA: Michael Olaf Montessori Company, 2013. Print.

Teachers and Students of Mountain Laurel Montessori School. "Work of the Hand Through the Curriculum and Across the Planes of Development: A Compilation of Creative Ideas." Ed. David Kahn. *The NAMTA Journal* 38.2 (2013): 108–119. Print.

GIVING A FACE TO HUMANITY:
AN OVERVIEW OF MONTESSORI
PRIMARY GEOGRAPHY[166]

Introduction

From early childhood through adolescence, the study of geography is integral to Montessori's peaceful, child-centered method of education. In these troubling political times, geography education is more important than ever to foster diplomacy and understanding in order to diffuse conflicts rather than exacerbate them. Starting around three years of age, children in the Montessori Primary Casa, or "Children's House," are exposed to geography as an integrated component of their well-rounded education. The universal needs and commonalities of mankind, not contentious political issues, are the focus throughout the child's Montessori Primary years. Placing emphasis on universalities and cultural traditions lays a critical foundation for greater geographical understanding in the Elementary and Adolescent years.

Introduction to Montessori Primary Geography

Geography in the Montessori Primary Casa examines earth's physical features as well as world cultures. Starting around age three or three-and-a-half, an individual student with good self-control receives his first formal geography lesson with a

---

[166] This article includes edited excerpts from *Montessori Primary Terminology*, © 2016, and *The Peace Table*, © 2015, by Mary Da Prato. *Montessori Primary Terminology* is both a reference and a glossary of terms used in the Montessori Primary prepared environment. It also contains a list of Primary presentations and the general order in which they are presented. *The Peace Table* emphasizes Montessori's comprehensive peace education curriculum and conflict resolution practices for children approximately three through six years of age.

manipulative known as the "Sandpaper Globe."

Sandpaper Globe

The Sandpaper Globe is a small globe depicting the distribution of earth's land and water. This manipulative helps children distinguish between land and water formations on earth. Land is represented by sandpaper, which students are encouraged to touch and feel. Water is represented by smooth blue paint. By touching the rough and smooth portions of the Sandpaper Globe, young children receive a hands-on impression of the difference between land and water. At this time, the guide (teacher) introduces the vocabulary "land" and "water" and has the child touch and trace examples of both on the Sandpaper Globe.

Painted Globe

Following success with the Sandpaper Globe, the child is introduced to the "Painted Globe." The Painted Globe, which is the same size as the Sandpaper Globe, helps children learn the difference between continents and the ocean. The ocean is painted blue while continents are brightly painted in a variety of colors. With the guide's help, children learn to identify each continent by name in preparation for future geography work including "Land and Water Forms"[167] and "Puzzle Maps."[168] The activity Land and Water Forms continues to focus on earth's physical geography while Puzzle Maps introduce physical geography in conjunction

---

[167] A series of geography and vocabulary lessons, "Land and Water Forms" are models of earth's land and water formations including an island and a lake. For maximum clarity, each Land and Water Form model is generic rather than based upon an actual geographic location.

[168] A "Puzzle Map" is a wooden puzzle with knobbed pieces representing continents, countries, states, or provinces. Puzzle Maps are a hands-on geography and vocabulary activity as well as a catalyst for further geography studies.

with cultural geography. These two activities are presented parallel to one another.

Land and Water Forms

The activity Land and Water Forms helps students three-and-a-half to four years of age with prior "Geometry Cabinet"[169] experience learn how to identify and differentiate between and among various Land and Water Forms through models that isolate natural geographical features when water is poured over them. Two opposite Land and Water Forms, such as island and lake, are introduced simultaneously to concretely highlight their contrasting forms. The Land and Water Form pairs introduced in the Casa are as follows: island and lake, peninsula and gulf, and isthmus and straight. Land and Water Form pairs for cape and bay as well as system of lakes and archipelago (system of islands) may be presented at the guide's discretion.

Puzzle Maps

After learning the world's continents through hands-on work with the Painted Globe, children three-and-half years of age and older are introduced to several "Puzzle Maps" with knobbed pieces which provide further experience in world geography. Learning the names of each continent, country, and state or province represented by puzzle pieces expands the child's vocabulary and encourages dialogue about faraway places. In addition to acting as a catalyst for geography studies, Puzzle Maps foster awareness of spatial relationships. Knobs on the puzzle pieces also encourage use of the pencil grip, the proper hand position needed to eventually write by hand. There are eight required Puzzle Maps in the Primary

---

[169] The "Geometry Cabinet" is a drawered cabinet containing various geometric shapes including circles, squares, triangles, and polygons to feel and trace as a foundation for formal geometry studies in later years.

prepared environment: Puzzle Map of the World, a Puzzle Map for each inhabited continent (Africa, Asia, Europe, North America, Oceania, South America), and a Puzzle Map of the states or provinces of the country in which the Casa is located. Additional Puzzle Maps may be provided in the Casa at the guide's discretion. A brief explanation of each type of Puzzle Map officially presented in the Casa follows.

Puzzle Map of the World

The first Puzzle Map introduced in the Casa, the "Puzzle Map of the World" has knobbed puzzle pieces of each of the world's seven continents: Africa, Antarctica, Asia, Europe, North America, Oceania (Australia), and South America. Students three-and-a-half years of age are introduced to this geography activity following experience with the Painted Globe. Around this time, students may also be working with Land and Water Forms.

Puzzle Maps of Individual Continents

Students three-and-a-half to five years of age who have worked with the Puzzle Map of the World and can identify each of the seven continents by name receive their first presentation for "Puzzle Maps of Individual Continents." Each inhabited continent has its own Puzzle Map that is subdivided into countries. The first Continent Puzzle Map presented is typically the one that represents the location of the Casa, which may be called "Puzzle Map of the Home Continent." For example, if the classroom is located in North America, the Puzzle Map of North America is the first Continent Puzzle Map presented. Following experience with the Puzzle Map of the Home Continent, the other five Continent Puzzle Maps representing inhabited continents may be introduced one at a time in any order.

Puzzle Map of the Home Country

Following success with the Puzzle Map of the Home Continent, students three-and-a-half to four years of age are introduced to the "Puzzle Map of the Home Country." The Puzzle Map of the Home Country consists of knobbed puzzle pieces which represent the country's states or provinces. Hands-on experience with the Puzzle Map of the Home Country gives young learners a tangible geography experience in preparation for formal studies in later years. Names of states or provinces and their capital cities are introduced following hands-on exploration. Puzzle Maps of other countries and their states or provinces may be introduced at the guide's discretion.

Puzzle Map Extensions

Putting together Puzzle Maps and learning their accompanying vocabulary provides a foundation, not an end point, for a child's geography experience in the Casa. Knowing the names of oceans, continents, countries, states, and capitals without context is insufficient for fostering cultural awareness and understanding. Geographical vocabulary, while important, consists mainly of statements such as "This is Asia," or "The capital of Wyoming is Cheyenne." For a truly enriching geography experience, the guide uses Puzzle Maps as an entry point to age-appropriate cultural studies including art appreciation, art history, music appreciation, music history, and other topics of interest to young children through photographs, replicas of artifacts, and guests as well as recorded and live music.

An example of an age-appropriate cultural geography lesson could be a basic introduction to the history and culture of Impressionist art. Over the course of several days, the guide may introduce examples of Impressionist art and artists in her Casa to an individual child or small group of children with the help of a specific Puzzle Map, photographs, postcards, reproductions of fine art, and other visual aids to enhance appreciation of art from a different era and culture. To draw a connection between Impressionism and geography, the guide may bring out the Puzzle Map of Europe during one or several of her small group presentations and isolate the puzzle piece of France on the rug where the students are gathered as a tangible, visual aid to her lessons about the origins of Impressionist art and its cultural influences. While relating a brief history of Impressionism, the guide can bring her story back to the universality of art by saying something like, "Art has always been important to people all over the world. Although Impressionist art originated far away a long time ago and influenced other cultures, we can still enjoy looking at it today. Some artists living today are inspired by Impressionism when creating original artwork, even though the Impressionist movement took place many years ago." Using the Puzzle Maps and other visual aids in conjunction with age-appropriate oral history presentations helps cultivate global awareness in young children without resorting to lectures or treading upon controversial political issues. Instead of internalizing divisive politics and prejudices, children in the Casa concretely participate in universal human experiences such as art appreciation through the guide's cognitively appropriate, factual lessons that incorporate both the past and present to help lay the foundation for a more harmonious, peaceful future.

Further Exploration of Universalities

Everyone on earth, regardless of where they live, needs air, water, food, shelter, and love. These universal needs of mankind may be explored in simple picture books that show loving families from around the world caring for their children, providing them with the necessities of life. Once universalities are established, cultural differences regarding human necessities may be explored in an age-appropriate, politically neutral manner. For example, while everyone on earth needs to eat, the particular types of foods humans consume depend largely upon their physical surroundings, climate, and cultural environment. A guide may explain differences in diet due to climate and cultural traditions by showing photographs, telling factual oral stories, and reading picture books to small groups of students about what kinds of foods grow in specific places. Temperate climates, for instance, produce a different range of foods than those found in tropical climates. These types of lessons combine both physical and cultural geography in a factual, non-biased manner that expands young children's understanding of the wider world. For further sensorial exploration, the guide or a guest may also occasionally introduce foods from other places and cultures for students to sample during snack or lunchtime. Following the introduction of a new food, the guide can give basic history lessons to small groups of students about the food's origin, thereby creating a holistic presentation that includes history, geography, botany, biology, and cultural studies to expand the child's knowledge of the world beyond the Casa.

Geography Folders

In addition to Puzzle Maps and picture books, geography in the Casa is further explored through a set of materials called "Geography Folders" or "Picture Folders." Captioned pictures organized by continent into separate Geography Folders allow children to see glimpses of the world, its peoples, landmarks, buildings, flora, fauna, and geographic features including biomes such as deserts, oceans, tropical rainforests, and coral reefs. Pictures in the Geography Folders, which may include international postcards, travel photographs, and magazine clippings, provide a catalyst for spontaneous or guided discussions about cultures and places. There is one Geography Folder for each continent on earth including Antarctica as well as one Picture Folder for each Land and Water Formation studied in the Casa such as lakes, islands, peninsulas, and gulfs. While the external appearance of Geography Folders may vary by Casa, each folder in a given prepared environment follows a uniform style for ease of independent student use. For organizational purposes, many Casas make Geography Folders from plain manila envelopes labeled with a drawing or photograph of the continent or land and water formation represented. The Geography Folder for South America, for example, should have a photograph or drawing of South America on the front of the envelope either in one of the corners or in the center. All other Geography Folders should be labeled in the same manner for consistency. Between eight and fifteen pictures are in each folder at all times for student exploration. Geography Folder pictures are rotated occasionally to maintain student interest and encourage repeated use.

A child who has had a lesson in the Geography Folders may choose to look at the captioned pictures from one folder at a time when interested during his uninterrupted three hour work period for leisure and reading practice. Any picture in a Geography Folder can also be used by the guide as a visual aid for an individual or small group presentation about a particular culture, festival, or landmark depicted in the chosen photograph. Geography Folder pictures can also be used as a starting point to "Facilitated Conversations"[170] between a guide and an individual child or small group of students to promote language development and expand students' knowledge of the world. To lead a Facilitated Conversation with a single student, the guide chooses a picture from one of the Geography Folders, isolates it in front of the child on a table or rug, and then asks him a general, open-

---

[170] "Facilitated Conversations" are an official daily language activity performed with two-and-a-half through six year old children in the Montessori Primary prepared environment as a means of fostering optimal spoken language development in preparation for literacy and creative writing.

ended question such as, "What do you see in this picture?" How the guide continues her open-ended Facilitated Conversation depends upon the individual child's response to her general question about the photograph. If the picture is of a young child riding a bicycle, the student may say that he has a bicycle too, just like the one in the picture! Once the child has drawn a connection between the picture and himself, the guide may emphasize the universal nature of the activity depicted in the photograph by saying something like, "Yes, the girl in this picture is riding a bicycle. People ride bicycles in many parts of the world. Let's see where this picture is from." The guide may then flip the picture over to reveal its caption. If the child is literate, the guide invites him to read what it says. If the child cannot yet read, the guide reads the caption aloud as in, "This caption says, 'Beijing, China.' That's where this picture was taken." After reading the caption, the guide turns the photograph face-up again so the child can see it. Depending on the child's level of interest, the guide can create a more detailed geographic connection by inviting him to take out the Puzzle Map of Asia to locate the puzzle piece representing China. The guide may then place the puzzle piece of China next to the picture to draw a concrete connection between the two objects. How the lesson continues will depend heavily upon the child's cognitive development, level of interest, previous experiences with geography, and any spontaneous comments he makes about the subject. When a lull develops in the discussion, the guide may conclude the Facilitated Conversation by saying, "Thank you for having a conversation with me about this photograph. I am going to do some other work now. What would you like to do next?" If the child wants to continue to look at Geography Folder pictures independently, he is free to do so. The child may also invite a friend to have a conversation with him about pictures in the Geography Folder if he desires. There is also the possibility that the child may be inspired to work with the corresponding Puzzle Map after putting the Geography Folder materials away in their proper place in the Casa. If there are books about geography in the Reading Corner, the child may want to take a look at them. Cultural activities in the art section may also be available for the child's exploration. And of course, the child may be finished with geography for the present time and choose different work entirely. The beauty of the uninterrupted three hour work period is its flexibility and open-endedness that allows children to continue to explore introduced topics for as long or as little as desired following an initial presentation from the guide.

Conclusion

Like all other studies in the Montessori Primary classroom, geography is integrated within the Casa's holistic environment, available for independent student exploration at the moment of interest in lieu of an adult-imposed schedule. By treating geography in the same manner as other subjects in the Casa, the study of humanity and cultures becomes a natural, integral, and integrated part of the child's life that lays a foundation for positive human relations in the local community and abroad, an essential prerequisite to universal, lasting peace.[171]

References

Da Prato, Mary. *Montessori Primary Terminology*. Seattle: CreateSpace Independent Publishing Platform, 2016. Print.

Da Prato, Mary. *The Peace Table*. Seattle: CreateSpace Independent Publishing Platform, 2015. Print.

---

[171] Montessori, Maria. *The Child, Society, and the World: Unpublished Speeches and Writings*. Vol. 7. Oxford: Clio, 2006. Print. The Clio Montessori Ser. Pages 111-112.

Montessori, Maria. *The Child, Society, and the World: Unpublished Speeches and Writings*. Vol. 7. Oxford: Clio, 2006. Print. The Clio Montessori Ser.

THE OUTDOOR CLASSROOM: AN OVERVIEW OF MONTESSORI'S INTEGRATED CURRICULUM

It is no secret that in today's high-tech world, students are too often starved for meaningful interactions with nature.[172] In response to this problem, hands-on nature study as a scheduled part of the school day has recently re-emerged as an important component of children's holistic development.[173] But what these so-called nature education programs lack is a completely integrated approach wherein students, not teachers, control the amount of time spent each day on outdoor learning experiences.[174] [175] There is, in fact, one such educational method which is centered around student freedom of work choice both indoors and outdoors, and it has existed for more than one hundred years.[176]

The Montessori Method

Many people have heard the name "Montessori" but are unsure or confused about the method's child-centered philosophy, as well as how it relates to outdoor education. In brief, the Montessori Method is a scientific pedagogy based upon Dr. Maria Montessori's extensive observations of how children actually learn when free to pursue their own interests within a reasonably

---

[172] Louv, Richard. "Guest Editorial: The More High-Tech Our Schools Become, the More They Need Nature." *Science and Children* 49.7 (2012): 8-9. Web. 13 June 2017. 0-www.jstor.org.catalog.multcolib.org/stable/43747324.

[173] Eick, Charles J. "Use of the Outdoor Classroom and Nature-Study to Support Science and Literacy Learning: A Narrative Case Study of a Third-Grade Classroom." *Journal of Science Teacher Education* 23.7 (2012): 789-803. Web. 13 June 2017. <http://0-www.jstor.org.catalog.multcolib.org/stable/43156675>.

[174] Kahn, David. "Preface: Revelations Then and Now- Guided by Nature." *The NAMTA Journal* 38.1 (2013): 1-5. Print.

[175] O'Shaughnessy, Molly. "Epilogue: The Child and the Environment." *The NAMTA Journal* 38.1 (2013): 279-292. Print.

[176] Kahn, David. "Preface: Revelations Then and Now- Guided by Nature." *The NAMTA Journal* 38.1 (2013): 1-5. Print.

structured framework. In a Primary Casa, or mixed-age classroom for young children, two-and-a-half through six year old students are at liberty to choose their own educational activities provided they have received a lesson from the teacher, known as a "guide." Activities in both the indoor and outdoor prepared environments are selected and used during a minimum uninterrupted three hour work period each school day. In an authentic Montessori program, there are no school bells or other artificial demarcations of time designating when it is time to do mathematics, language, art, gardening, or any other subject. Recess, in the traditional sense, should be non-existent as students are free to work and play outside throughout the work period.[177]

Three Part Work Cycle

There is often disbelief or skepticism regarding how a system of schooling based upon student freedom of work choice can function properly, whether indoors or outdoors. How can there be a large degree of student choice without chaos? How can the teacher ensure that all the essential school subjects are covered? What if two or more students want to use the same material at the same time? To answer these questions, it is important to understand the framework which maintains order in every high-functioning Montessori classroom. This framework, known as the "Three Part Work Cycle," establishes the three essential rules of the prepared environment starting on the first day of school and continuing throughout the child's entire Montessori education:

1) A student may select any available material following an initial lesson from the teacher.

2) The student who has chosen an available material may

---

[177] O'Shaughnessy, Molly. "Epilogue: The Child and the Environment." *The NAMTA Journal* 38.1 (2013): 279-92. Print.

work with it for as long as he desires during the classroom's minimum three hour uninterrupted work period.

3) When finished using a material, the student must return it to its proper location in the classroom in its original condition so it is ready for the next child to use.

These three rules help prevent conflicts among students, keep children engaged in their freely chosen activities in every subject area, and give the guide ample opportunity to frequently present new lessons or "presentations" to individual or small groups of students. To ensure students learn essential skills, the guide observes each child's needs and interests in order to create presentations in every subject area which are irresistibly appealing. An effective means of fostering student learning followed by purposeful independent exploration is to incorporate the classroom's outdoor prepared environment.

The Outdoor Classroom

In an authentic Montessori program, there is no distinction between the indoor classroom and its adjacent outdoor prepared environment.[178] Also known as the "outdoor classroom," the outdoor prepared environment exists as a natural extension of the indoor classroom. Unlike a typical playground which is used as a break from schoolwork during a designated recess period determined by the teacher or school, the Montessori outdoor classroom is designed to enrich students' holistic learning experiences. Obvious uses of the outdoor classroom include hands-on lessons in nature study. What better place is there for students to plant flower bulbs, observe bees at work, and identify various

---

[178] Kahn, David. "Preface: Revelations Then and Now- Guided by Nature." *The NAMTA Journal* 38.1 (2013): 1-5. Print.

types of birds and leaf shapes? There are also less obvious uses for the outdoor classroom including taking various academic materials outside during nice weather. Language arts and mathematics, for example, can be completed outdoors just as well as indoors. In fact, working with academic materials in conjunction with nature can enhance comprehension in various subject areas.[179] When weather conditions permit, the prepared outdoor environment is also an excellent place for art activities such as finger painting on dampened paper on a small table or tempera painting on paper clipped to an easel. In short, the Montessori outdoor classroom can be the setting for almost any activity presented in the indoor classroom.

Order in the Outdoor Classroom

There are only a few rules when it comes to use of the Montessori outdoor classroom. First, the child must be appropriately dressed for the weather. When children enter the indoor classroom at the beginning of the school day, they are required to hang up their own coats and other outerwear such as hats and scarves in a designated area of the room. If a student wishes to use the adjacent outdoor classroom, permission from an adult is not required, but he must dress for the weather. The guide's assistant ensures that students are appropriately attired before going outside. If a student goes outside on a cold day without wearing a coat, the assistant gently intervenes by saying something like, "Brr! It's awfully cold outside today! Let's go get your coat and hat." The assistant then leads the child back into the indoor classroom to retrieve the coat and hat. Once dressed for the weather, the child is free to return to the safe outdoor classroom at will. Students in both the indoor and outdoor classrooms are supervised by an adult at all times.

---

[179] Vaz, Nimal. "Montessori Special Education and Nature's Playground." *The NAMTA Journal* 38.1 (2013): 71-79. Print.

Second, the rules of the Three Part Work Cycle apply to the outdoor classroom just as they do in the indoor classroom. A student working outside may choose any available material suitable for outdoor use following a presentation from the guide. The student may then work with that material as long as desired during the work period. Finally, the student must return the material to its proper location in its original condition when finished. If the current weather conditions would ruin a particular indoor material, the guide or assistant intervenes to tell the child why the material must be used in the indoor classroom that day, and enforces that limitation. Generally, the material may be moved to the outdoor classroom, weather permitting.

Connections between the Indoor and Outdoor Classrooms

There are Montessori exercises designed exclusively for outdoor use, such as raking leaves, as well as activities which may be completed indoors or outdoors during good weather, such as looking at a picture book. But there are also exercises which bridge the indoor and outdoor classrooms to create optimal, hands-on learning experiences. Some of these activities, including the "Botany Cabinet," a cabinet filled with leaf shaped puzzle pieces, are universal to all authentic Montessori programs. Other activities, such as those related to food preparation, vary from school to school based upon the local and regional culture as well as the guide's own preferences and observations of student interests. Like many aspects of Montessori education, connections between the indoor and outdoor prepared learning environments are fluid and open-ended.

Botany Cabinet

Starting around four years of age, children in the Primary classroom receive presentations with the "Botany Cabinet" or "Leaf Shape Cabinet." The Botany Cabinet is a "manipulative," or Montessori educational material, which uses knobbed wooden puzzle pieces of leaf shapes to introduce leaf shape identification as a precursor to formal botany study in later years. Leaf shape puzzle pieces are stored in thin drawers in a box resembling a small cabinet. Typically six leaf shape puzzle pieces are stored in each drawer for a total of approximately fourteen to eighteen different leaf shapes. The materials in the Botany Cabinet are used for a number of official Montessori presentations as well as several related activities well-suited for the outdoor prepared environment.

During the first Botany Cabinet presentation, the guide isolates three leaf shape puzzle pieces on a table. For maximum clarity, the guide deliberately chooses three leaf shapes which contrast in appearance, such as "ovate," "linear," and "hastate." After isolating the three leaf shapes, the guide picks up one of the leaf shapes by its knob with the non-dominant hand using the pencil grip (index and middle fingers on top with the thumb supporting the grip underneath). The guide then traces the outline of the leaf shape in midair using a pointer, such as a chopstick or orange stick, with the dominant hand. Following this demonstration, the guide returns the leaf shape and pointer to the table. The child is then encouraged to carefully repeat the guide's tracing motions using the same leaf shape and pointer. Holding the leaf shape with the pencil grip and tracing it with the pointer in the prescribed manner exercises precise fine motor movements which provide an indirect preparation for writing. The guide repeats the process of tracing a leaf shape and giving the child a turn until all three leaf shapes on the table have been traced. Once all three leaf shapes have been traced, the child is free to trace the shapes in any one drawer at a time. When the child is more experienced, he is invited to trace the leaf shapes from any two drawers at a time, followed by all three drawers.

Following the initial Botany Cabinet presentation, the guide presents a number of follow-up activities to expand and solidify knowledge. These activities may include tracing leaf shape puzzle pieces onto paper to further exercise fine motor coordination, learning the names of the leaf shapes to lay a foundation for nature study, and matching leaf shape puzzle pieces to leaf outlines printed on cards to aid with visual discrimination of various forms in preparation for reading. Outdoor related activities for the Botany Cabinet may include matching leaf shape puzzle pieces to real leaves in the environment, making leaf rubbings, photograph paper contact prints, pressed leaves, and simple botany lessons appropriate for the individual student's level of cognitive maturity.

Additional Outdoor Experiences

In addition to identifying leaf shapes, Primary students also learn how to grow and care for plants. One enjoyable technique for potting plants is to use a paper pot maker tool, which allows students to create biodegradable flower pots out of recycled newspaper. This ingenious device is available for purchase online through a number of online vendors including Montessori Services at www.montessoriservices.com. Another favorite activity for Montessori children is creating compost to help nourish the garden. A number of Montessori classrooms encourage the recycling of organic matter, such as banana peels, by placing a small compost container either in the classroom kitchen or just outside the door to the outdoor classroom environment. After lunch, or at the end of the school day, the small compost container is emptied into the outdoor environment's compost. In addition to providing good soil for plants, the compost area is an excellent place for students to study worms at work as they churn up the soil. To reinforce children's hands-on outdoor learning, the guide may read factual picture books about flowers, worms, beneficial bugs, and other aspects of nature. Like many other facets of Montessori education, follow-up presentations for outdoor experiences are open-ended and based upon the guide's observations of current student needs and interests.

Going Out

A fully integrated outdoor prepared environment is a crucial feature of Montessori education that does not disappear after a child's Primary years. On the contrary, during a child's Montessori Elementary years from ages six through twelve, meaningful outdoor access at will becomes increasingly vital for the maturing student's optimal holistic development.[180] In addition to having an adjacent outdoor classroom like their younger peers, Montessori Elementary students also gain access to a Montessori practice known as "Going Out." Unlike a traditional field trip in which all students in class must attend on the teacher's schedule, Going Out allows children to arrange research expeditions in supervised small groups outside of the school grounds. For example, if a small group of students is studying plants in the Rosaceac family, they may want to visit an orchard, rose test garden, or botanical garden in order to further their research. Since students in other groups are likely working on completely different projects, as is common in Montessori Elementary,[181] a whole-class field trip would not satisfy every student's research needs. Instead, a group of students working on a particular project makes a proposal for the teacher outlining the purposes, costs, transportation, time, and supervision that their Going Out trip would entail.[182] Planning for outings in

---

[180] Leonard, Gerard. "Deepening Cosmic Education." *The NAMTA Journal* 38.1 (2013): 135-44. Print.

[181] *Collaborative Learning*. Dir. Emily Green. Perf. Kay Baker, Allyn Travis, and Phyllis Pottish-Lewis. Montessori Guide, 2014. Web. 7 July 2017. <http://montessoriguide.org/elementary-age-work/>.

this manner is an essential life skill that Montessori Elementary students continually hone in preparation for purposeful independent trips during adolescence and eventually adulthood.[183]

The Outdoor Environment at Home

When creating a prepared outdoor environment for your child at home, safety is paramount. Make sure to supervise your child at all times. Also be mindful of the climate. If the climate calls for coats, hats, or other outdoor accessories, create a place in your home where your child can access outerwear with minimal adult assistance. You can do this by providing a wall peg at the child's level to facilitate retrieving a coat and putting it away independently to foster functional independence. To help keep dirt and mud from tracking in the house, consider placing a boot scraper outside near the door. Provide child-sized garden tools such as a rake, shovel, watering can, and trowel so your child can be purposefully involved in garden care. Grow plants together and model care by using correct amounts of water and fertilizer. Provide a compost container to help nourish what you have planted. The specific plants and garden activities you provide will be highly dependent upon the climate and size of your outdoor environment. If you live in an apartment, consider container gardening or hydroponics. When unsure what to plant and how to provide proper plant care, consult your local plant nursery.

In addition to child-sized garden tools, consider adding a sandbox or sand and water table for creative play under supervision. Also provide water features such as birdbaths, fountains, and ponds. A sundial is another fun addition to the garden, and can spark conversations about how people used to tell

---

[182] *Going Out*. Dir. Emily Green. Perf. Phyllis Pottish-Lewis, Kay Baker, and Allyn Travis. Montessori Guide, 2014. Web. 1 July 2017. <http://montessoriguide.org/elementary-education>.
[183] Ibid.

time before there were clocks.[184] An excellent resource for additional outdoor environment ideas is Molly Dannenmaier's *A Child's Garden: 60 Ideas to Make Any Garden Come Alive for Children*.[185] Do not be deterred by its publication date. Despite being a decade old, *A Child's Garden* is a timeless reference for families who want to create enchanting outdoor environments for their children. No matter which garden designs and features you ultimately implement, remember to use common sense and supervise your child for safety at all times.

Conclusion

As our world continues to become increasingly technology-based, it is more important than ever that children do not lose contact with nature, the growth process, and the outdoors. Young children in particular need hands-on experiences with the outdoors in order to learn how things grow, where their food comes from, and the importance of conserving nature so that future generations can enjoy its wonders.[186] A brief recess period on the teacher's schedule is hardly sufficient, especially when that recess period focuses upon artificial play structures in stark play areas devoid of flora and fauna.[187] What children need is a school system in which they can seamlessly move between carefully prepared indoor and outdoor environments throughout the day to support optimal holistic development. This system of freely chosen indoor and

---

[184] "Sundial." *Encyclopædia Britannica*. Web. 7 July 2017. <http://library.eb.com.wccls.idm.oclc.org/levels/referencecenter/article/sundial/70362>.

[185] Dannenmaier, Molly. *A Child's Garden: 60 Ideas to Make Any Garden Come Alive for Children*. Portland: Timber, 2008. Print.

[186] Verschuur, Mary B. "Ecosystems in the Backyard: Preparing a Diverse Outdoor Environment for Primary (Ages Three to Six) Children." *The NAMTA Journal* 38, no. 1 (Winter 2013): 61-65.

[187] Chawla, Louise. "Bonding with the Natural World: The Roots of Environmental Awareness." *The NAMTA Journal* 38.1 (2013): 39-51. Print.

outdoor work thankfully already exists in authentic Montessori schools throughout the country and the world. As adults, we merely need to expand its implementation to help lay a foundation for a better future.

References

Chawla, Louise. "Bonding with the Natural World: The Roots of Environmental Awareness." *The NAMTA Journal* 38.1 (2013): 39-51. Print.

Collaborative Learning. Dir. Emily Green. Perf. Kay Baker, Allyn Travis, and Phyllis Pottish-Lewis. Montessori Guide, 2014. Web. 7 July 2017. <http://montessoriguide.org/elementary-age-work/>.

Dannenmaier, Molly. *A Child's Garden: 60 Ideas to Make Any Garden Come Alive for Children*. Portland: Timber, 2008. Print.

Eick, Charles J. "Use of the Outdoor Classroom and Nature-Study to Support Science and Literacy Learning: A Narrative Case Study of a Third-Grade Classroom." *Journal of Science Teacher Education* 23.7 (2012): 789-803. Web. 13 June 2017. <http://0-www.jstor.org.catalog.multcolib.org/stable/43156675>.

Going Out. Dir. Emily Green. Perf. Phyllis Pottish-Lewis, Kay Baker, and Allyn Travis. Montessori Guide, 2014. Web. 1 July 2017. <http://montessoriguide.org/elementary-education>.

Kahn, David. "Preface: Revelations Then and Now- Guided by Nature." *The NAMTA Journal* 38.1 (2013): 1-5. Print.

Leonard, Gerard. "Deepening Cosmic Education." *The NAMTA Journal* 38.1 (2013): 135-44. Print.

Louv, Richard. "Guest Editorial: The More High-Tech Our Schools Become, the More They Need Nature." *Science and Children* 49.7 (2012): 8-9. Web. 13 June 2017. <http://0-www.jstor.org.catalog.multcolib.org/stable/43747324>.

O'Shaughnessy, Molly. "Epilogue: The Child and the Environment." *The NAMTA Journal* 38.1 (2013): 279-292. Print.

"Sundial." *Encyclopædia Britannica.* Web. 7 July 2017. <http://library.eb.com.wccls.idm.oclc.org/levels/referencecenter/article/sundial/70362>.

Vaz, Nimal. "Montessori Special Education and Nature's Playground." *The NAMTA Journal* 38.1 (2013): 71-79. Print.

Verschuur, Mary B. "Ecosystems in the Backyard: Preparing a Diverse Outdoor Environment for Primary (Ages Three to Six) Children." *The NAMTA Journal* 38, no. 1 (Winter 2013): 61-65.

PARENT INVOLVEMENT:
A MONTESSORI PERSPECTIVE

From preschool to K-8 programs, Montessori is entering public school districts across the country at an increasing rate.[188] There are now more than 500 public, charter, and magnet Montessori programs serving approximately 125,000 students and counting.[189] This growing educational movement of Montessori in the public sector can leave parents confused about their role in the classroom as well as outside it. Families with children enrolled in a Montessori program often feel frustrated or hurt when their volunteer activities are typically restricted to behind-the-scenes work rather than directly presenting projects in the classroom. Despite misconceptions about parental involvement, family participation is at the core of the Montessori philosophy starting before the first day of school and continuing throughout the child's Montessori school years, and sometimes beyond.

Before a child is enrolled in a Montessori program, it helps to have a basic understanding of the curriculum so parents know what to expect. Montessori is a scientific, child-centered pedagogy based upon over one hundred years of direct observation of the natural needs, behaviors, and interests of children in every social and economic class all over the world.[190] In accordance with these observations, an authentic Montessori classroom includes the following critical elements: 1) the trained Montessori guide (teacher), 2) a developmentally appropriate mixed-age group of students, 3) a complete array of official manipulatives (classroom materials), and 4) a minimum uninterrupted three hour work period

---

[188] For the latest public Montessori news, visit www.montessoripublic.org.

[189] "Public Montessori." *Montessori Public*. National Center for Montessori in the Public Sector, 2018. Web. 02 Apr. 2018.
<https://www.montessoripublic.org/>.

[190] Montessori, Maria. *The Absorbent Mind*. Vol. 1. Oxford: Clio, 2004. Print. The Clio Montessori Ser. Page 185.

in which students may choose any available manipulative or activity that has been previously presented by the guide during an individual or small group lesson. The combination of these elements constitutes "the prepared environment."

To maintain a calm atmosphere that supports student concentration, parent interactions within the prepared environment are carefully regulated. Instead of presenting lessons, which is the role of the trained Montessori guide (teacher), parents are invited to observe children at work in the classroom unobtrusively. There are typically two ways in which a parent observation may occur depending upon the setup of an individual Montessori school. Some Montessori schools have a one-way mirror for parents to observe how the classroom functions when no guests are present. For this type of observation, it helps to have a staff member nearby to answer any questions the parent may have about the lessons being presented or why a child is working with a manipulative in a particular fashion. The second, and more common, type of observation is a scheduled visit in the classroom. Before a classroom observation, the parent is briefed on behavioral expectations. To help preserve the authenticity of the prepared environment and to avoid causing unnecessary disruptions, the observer is usually expected to sit on a chair silently in the corner of the classroom, not interacting with students. Some classrooms may have a special "observer chair" or "observation chair" designated for this purpose. From the observation chair, the adult is expected to take notes, stay seated for the duration of the observation, remain as unobtrusive as possible, and keep interactions with children and staff to a minimum. If a child approaches you, smile and nicely tell them you are busy working. Resume taking notes in silence until the child finds other work. It is important to note that the Montessori policy of silent observation is not meant to be uninviting. Rather, by keeping the parent observer at the periphery of the classroom, children are less likely to be distracted from their work. Having low-key observations also gives the parent the opportunity to see how the classroom normally functions.

The idea of sitting quietly in the corner of the room during an observation can be a put-off to many parents who are used to being directly involved. But scheduled observations are only one portion of parent involvement in a Montessori program. Volunteering to prepare and maintain classroom supplies and equipment requested by the guide outside of the classroom is another way to support your child. This may involve filling paint bottles, cutting paper, or shopping for baking supplies outside of class time. Always ask your child's teacher before deciding to volunteer or donating supplies for a project. What may be commonplace in a traditional school, such as selecting reading materials for the classroom, may not be in alignment with a Montessori teacher's classroom needs or school policy.

In addition to observing in the classroom and preparing materials outside of class, parents are strongly encouraged to attend parent nights to learn more about the Montessori Method and what they can do at home to reinforce in-class studies and expectations. In private Montessori schools, parent nights are often required. Topics and frequency of parent nights vary by school. Examples of parent night presentations may include "The Importance of Practical Life Skills," "Mathematics in the Classroom," and "Botany in the Early Years." Parent nights are typically presented by the child's teacher, whose presentations may include a slideshow followed by a question and answer period. For clarity, the teacher may also demonstrate the use of one of the classroom's manipulatives. How the teacher decides to present a particular topic depends upon a combination of school policies, personal preference, and observation of matters that need to be addressed in a particular school community. For the sake of maintaining privacy, concerns about individual students are not addressed at this time. To help keep families informed of their child's progress and areas that need attention, the teacher holds regular parent-teacher conferences in private. If parents have additional questions or concerns outside of a parent night or parent-teacher conference, they should follow the school protocol and make a discreet inquiry privately.

For parents who desire more direct involvement in their child's classroom activities, there are a number of options that may be available depending upon the particular Montessori school. A popular way to interact with your child in the classroom is to attend a "Parent-Child Work Day" or "Parent-Child Work Time." Usually held after school once per month or once every two weeks, a Parent-Child Work Time allows parents and significant others to visit their child's classroom to see examples of class work and presentations. During a Parent-Child Work Time, a child may decide to demonstrate favorite activities to family members, or take them on a guided tour of the classroom. Visitors are free to ask questions, but Parent-Child Work Time is the child's opportunity to shine. So if you attend a Parent-Child Work Time, be relaxed and flexible about what your child chooses to show you. Be supportive and respectful if your child demonstrates a presentation. Refrain from criticism or excessive praise as Montessori's philosophy is to foster learning and exploration as joyful, intrinsically rewarding experiences. Above all, have fun interacting with your child during these special events.

If you have a special skill, such as playing a musical instrument or folding origami, ask your child's teacher if you may schedule a brief presentation in the classroom. With children ages two-and-a-half to six in the Primary classroom, it is best to keep presentations brief to accommodate short attention spans, no more than ten minutes maximum. Elementary students may be able to handle a slightly longer presentation. Keep in mind that students in a Montessori classroom are free to attend individual and small group presentations at will, so do not feel hurt if only some of the children choose to participate in your planned activity. Younger children in particular may be inclined to come and go quietly during a presentation, which is also allowed.

Parents who want additional involvement with student activities during school hours may want to consider becoming chaperones for Montessori Elementary students ages six through twelve who are participating in a Montessori exercise called "Going Out." Instead of traditional field trips, small groups of Montessori Elementary students who are studying a particular topic of interest are free to create a proposal for a research trip. A group of students who are studying marine life, for example, may want to create a proposal for their teacher asking to go to a local aquarium during the school day to supplement their in-class and library studies. These frequent Going Out excursions, which vary considerably based upon student interests at a given time, require adult chaperones. Parents of Montessori Elementary students can be excellent candidates for this task. Even if your child is a Primary student not yet ready for Montessori Elementary, becoming a Going Out chaperone can be a wonderful opportunity to support older students in their educational endeavors while simultaneously learning about the kinds of Going Out trips your child may take in later school years.

In addition to direct involvement with student activities, many parent volunteers are needed outside of the classroom to help their school run smoothly. Auction projects, fundraising campaigns, alumni events, and newsletter writing are only some of the ways a Montessori school may encourage further family participation. An established Montessori school may also have a need for designated parent liaisons to facilitate communication between families and school staff.

Parents can also create a prepared environment at home to complement their child's classroom experiences. Providing a calm atmosphere at home in alignment with Montessori's child-centered philosophy is a task no less vital than involvement at your child's school. Examples of at-home measures may include providing open shelving rather than toy boxes to support a child's sense of order, having children keep their activities contained on a small table or rug to prevent clutter, and growing plants together to experience the wonder of nature. Being organized with open shelving for storage as well as involving your child in cooking, cleanup, and pet care under adult supervision helps instill responsibility, self-management, and independence. For additional activity and organization ideas for young children, consider reading *How to Raise an Amazing Child the Montessori Way* by Tim Seldin, *Montessori Play and Learn* by Lesley Britton, and *Child of the World: Montessori, Global Education for Age 3-12+* by Susan Mayclin Stephenson. Look for these titles and others at your local public library. Or, as another parent project, ask if you can help your child's school create a family lending library for the benefit of your community. During parent nights and parent-teacher conferences, be proactive in asking for specific ideas about how to support your child's learning at home.

Parent involvement practices in a Montessori school may be unfamiliar at first, but be assured that family support is integral to a high-functioning Montessori environment. Both at home and at school, parents are vital to their child's holistic development. No matter if you are observing in the classroom, attending parent events, being a chaperone, leading a fundraiser, or doing a combination of all of the above, your participation in Montessori school life matters. So speak with your child's Montessori teacher today. You never know what important undertakings await you in assisting your child and community for optimal development.

References

Britton, Lesley. *Montessori Play and Learn: A Parents Guide to Purposeful Pay from Two to Six*. New York: Crown Publishers, Inc., 1992.

Montessori, Maria. *The Absorbent Mind*. Vol. 1. Oxford: Clio, 2004. Print. The Clio Montessori Ser.

"Public Montessori." *Montessori Public*. National Center for Montessori in the Public Sector, 2018. Web. 02 Apr. 2018. <https://www.montessoripublic.org/>.

Seldin, Tim. *How to Raise an Amazing Child the Montessori Way: A Parent's Guide to Building Creativity, Confidence, and Independence*. 2nd ed. New York: Dorling Kindersley, 2017. Print.

Stephenson, Susan M. *Child of the World: Montessori, Global Education for Age 3-12+*. Arcata, CA: Michael Olaf Montessori Company, 2013. Print.

BECOMING PART OF THE PARADIGM SHIFT: THE CASE FOR MONTESSORI TRAINING[191]

With more than a one hundred year history of worldwide success, Montessori education is increasingly becoming part of the American public school landscape. According to the National Center for Montessori in the Public Sector, there are now more than 450 public Montessori schools in the United States.[192] Although Montessori accounts for only a small number of public schools in our nation, the creation of new Montessori public schools and the conversion of traditional classrooms into Montessori prepared environments are growing trends. This year alone,[193] Detroit Public Schools Community District has decided to open seven Montessori classrooms in response to community needs.[194] Public Montessori classrooms have also opened this year in Steamboat Springs, Colorado[195] and Racine, Wisconsin.[196] In Portland, Oregon, the state's first public Montessori preschool,

---

[191] This article was originally written in 2016. As of 2018, there are now more than 500 public, charter, and magnet Montessori schools in the United States which serve approximately 125,000 schools and counting. For updated information about public Montessori schools, visit www.montessoripublic.org.

[192] "National Center for Montessori in the Public Sector." *National Center for Montessori in the Public Sector*. The National Center for Montessori in the Public Sector, 2018. Web. 4 Apr. 2018. <http://www.public-montessori.org/>.

[193] "This year" throughout the article refers to 2016, the year this article was originally written.

[194] Einhorn, Erin. "Detroit Public Schools Try to Lure Skeptical Families by Adding Montessori Programs." *Chalkbeat*. Chalkbeat, 11 Aug. 2016. Web. 11 Aug. 2016. <http://www.chalkbeat.org/posts/detroit/2016/08/11/detroit-public-schools-try-lure-skeptical-families-adding-montessori-programs/>.

[195] Ristow, Teresa. "First Day of School for Mountain Village Montessori." *Steamboat Today*. Steamboat Pilot & Today, 6 Sept. 2016. Web. 6 Sept. 2016. <http://www.steamboattoday.com/news/2016/sep/06/first-day-school-mountain-village-montessori/>.

[196] "Montessori Program." Racine Unified School District, 2016. Web. 5 Oct. 2016. <http://www.rusd.org/montessori>.

Alder Montessori, has just begun its second school year.[197] Plans for opening Bend, Oregon's first Montessori public charter school in 2017 are currently underway.[198] [199] Similar reports of Montessori public and charter school applications continue to trickle into local media. As a public school teacher in a rapidly changing world, you may suddenly find your school district becoming part of the growing Montessori movement. But what exactly is Montessori education, and how will it affect you? To answer these questions, it is important to understand the history of the Montessori Method and its founder Dr. Maria Montessori.

Dr. Maria Montessori, a physician, founded her first school for three through six year old children in Italy in 1907. Through her careful scientific observations, Dr. Montessori concluded that children learn best when they freely choose their educational activities during an uninterrupted three hour work period in a prepared classroom environment. In Montessori pedagogy, a prepared environment consists of a mixed-age group of peers, an appropriate variety of sequentially designed educational materials known as "manipulatives," and a teacher or "guide" who is specifically trained to observe children and present materials appropriate for each individual student's developmental needs and desires as they occur. For the remainder of her life, Dr. Montessori continued to hone and expand her scientific pedagogy to include

---

[197] Stocco, Nicholas. "Alder Montessori to Receive Preschool Promise Funding." *Montessori Northwest*. Montessori Northwest, 23 Sept. 2016. Web. 23 Sept. 2016. <http://montessori-nw.org/blog/alder-montessori-to-receive-preschool-promise-funding>.

[198] Fisicaro, Kailey. "Montessori Charter School Approved for Bend." *The Bulletin*. Bend, Oregon: A Western Communications Company, 28 Sept. 2016. Web. 28 Sept. 2016. <http://www.bendbulletin.com/localstate/education/4695067-151/montessori-charter-school-approved-for-bend>.

[199] Desert Sky Montessori Charter School for grades K-3 is now operational. One grade will be added per year to make a K-8 school. For more information, visit their website at http://dsmontessori.org.

children from birth through twelve years of age, and described plans for how her method could be applied to twelve through eighteen year old students. While perfecting her child-centered educational method, Dr. Montessori travelled the world as a lecturer, wrote books, gave interviews, and led international teacher training courses to preserve her life's work for future generations. Eventually, "Montessori" became a public domain name, so Dr. Montessori founded Association Montessori Internationale (AMI) in 1929 to establish authentic Montessori teacher training courses that were true to her philosophy, pedagogy, and findings. Other respected Montessori organizations based upon Dr. Montessori's principles include American Montessori Society (AMS), Pan American Montessori Society (PAMS), and St. Nicholas Montessori. Today, thanks to Dr. Montessori's decades of advocacy for all children, the Montessori Method continues to thrive on every inhabited continent, reaching diverse students of all races and socio-economic backgrounds.[200] Now that Montessori education is gradually entering select public school systems in the United States, you can become part of a growing, time-honored, international movement that strives to help all children reach their fullest potentials.

Before adopting the Montessori Method, it is important to be aware of a few key facts. First, the name Montessori is public domain, meaning any individual or school can call itself a Montessori school without obtaining permission or a seal of approval from any organization. To ensure you are prepared to teach in an authentic Montessori classroom setting, you will need official Montessori training. Just like traditional education, Montessori pedagogy is not a matter of reading a few theory books and calling yourself an expert. Any information you may have obtained during your traditional teacher education course years is

---

[200] "The Origins." *AMI/USA*. AMI/USA, 2014. Web. 3 Apr. 2018. <http://amiusa.org/the-origins/>.

insufficient to fully understand and implement Montessori's scientific, child-centered pedagogy that has almost nothing in common with a traditional school, public or private, making official Montessori training essential. Montessori training is an oral tradition passed down to students by highly knowledgeable trainers with years of experience. Teacher trainers give lectures, demonstrate how to present lessons to children, and oversee hands-on practice with precisely designed manipulatives provided in the training center. Theory lectures and hands-on work with manipulatives are followed by practice teaching sessions. During practice teaching, students training to become Montessori guides work with children in a prepared classroom environment under the guidance of a skilled Montessori teacher. Although there are a number of Montessori training courses in the country and around the world which are based upon Dr. Montessori's findings, such as AMS, PAMS, and St. Nicholas, you may want to seriously consider obtaining an AMI Diploma as Association Montessori Internationale is the original Montessori training program that was founded by Dr. Maria Montessori.[201]

A second equally important point is that Montessori education is divided into developmentally appropriate, well-balanced, mixed-age groups for optimal social development. In authentic Montessori education, three through six year children attend "Primary Montessori," which is also known as the "Children's House" or "Casa," the Italian word for "house." The Montessori Primary Casa is not preschool, nor is it kindergarten. Instead, children as young as two years and ten months of age and as old as seven years of age work, learn, play, and interact with one another, each learning at their own pace. The four main subject areas taught in the Casa are Practical Life (life skills), Sensorial (the five senses and their attributes), Language (spoken language, writing, reading, and grammar), and Mathematics (counting, addition, subtraction,

---

[201] Ibid.

multiplication, and division into the thousands and possibly millions). Cultural activities, often referred to as "Cultural Extensions," include art, music, dance, botany, and geography. Cultural Extensions are holistically integrated within Practical Life, Sensorial, Language, and Mathematics for optimal, well-rounded learning. Different from a traditional preschool or daycare experience, graduating six or seven year old students from an authentic Montessori Children's House program are generally well-versed in social skills, personal care, and academics. Due to the precisely designed, sequential materials presented within a pro-social classroom environment, it is expected that graduating students will be eager, self-directed, self-regulated learners who read and write in legible cursive as well as understand how to add, subtract, multiply, and divide numbers into the thousands and possibly millions. Children who leave the Casa with this level of social development and academic achievement are clearly prepared to enter the first or second grade upon matriculation, not kindergarten. Unfortunately, due to funding issues in public schools and unawareness of the benefits of a Montessori foundation, it is seldom possible to implement an authentic Montessori Primary classroom for three through six year old students in order to achieve optimal outcomes. To ensure a mixed-age group of Primary school peers, a few public Montessori schools offer tuition-based Montessori for three and four year old students until public funding is granted upon a child turning five. This eliminates the opportunity for low-income families to benefit from a full Montessori experience. By starting Montessori Primary school at age five like in a traditional kindergarten, children miss approximately two-thirds of the sequential curriculum which is designed to build upon prior learning beginning at two years and ten months of age or three years of age.

In addition to Montessori Primary, there are also Montessori Elementary schools, some of which are in the public sector. Authentic Montessori Elementary training gives you the essential foundation to work with six through twelve year old children in a Montessori setting. The "Lower Elementary" classroom serves children ages six through nine while the "Upper Elementary" classroom serves children ages nine through twelve. In traditional school terms, this means that a Montessori Lower Elementary teacher will typically have a mixed-age group of first through third grade students in the same classroom while a Montessori Upper Elementary teacher will have a well-balanced group of fourth through sixth grade students in the same classroom. There are also Montessori Elementary programs that have six through twelve year old children, or first through sixth grade students, integrated in the same classroom like the one-room schoolhouses of the past. Like their younger counterparts, Montessori Elementary students ages six through twelve freely choose their activities throughout the day following a lesson or "presentation" from the guide. To ensure that elementary children are learning essential skills in all subject areas as well as meeting state grade level requirements, the guide helps students take personal responsibility for their learning by having them record their daily activities in a personal notebook. Using student notebooks as a guide, the teacher then meets with each student individually on a weekly or biweekly basis to assess progress and design appropriate lesson plans[202] in order to meet or exceed benchmarks in every subject area.[203]

Although rare, Montessori programs for students over twelve years of age exist. Twelve through eighteen year old adolescents are part of a program known as "Erdkinder," which is German for "earth children." Traditionally, Montessori education for adolescents has been centered around rural life to give students the

---

[202] Nielsen, Melinda, and AMI/USA. "The Three Essential Tools." *Montessori Guide*. Association Montessori Internationale of the United States, Inc., 2017. Web. 4 Apr. 2018. <http://montessoriguide.org/the-three-essential-tools/>.
[203] "AMI Montessori and the Common Core State Standards." *AMI/USA*. AMI/USA, 2014. Web. 5 Oct. 2016. <https://amiusa.org/ami-montessori-and-the-common-core-state-standards/>.

opportunity to explore the great outdoors as well as various trades including agriculture and inn keeping. Today, there are also urban Montessori adolescent programs to help meet the needs of city students living in our constantly changing, technologically advanced 21st century.[204]

Once you have decided which age group you would like to work or continue to work with, it is time to locate a Montessori training center. A current list of AMI training centers is available online at https://montessori-ami.org/training-programmes/training-courses. At this time, it is possible to take courses in Assistance to Infancy for working with children up to three years of age, Primary for teaching children ages three through six, and Elementary for teaching children ages six through twelve. An official course for teaching adolescents ages twelve through eighteen is still being designed,[205] but an AMI endorsed class held by the North American Montessori Teachers' Association (NAMTA) is available in the meantime.[206] There is also an AMI Inclusive Education Course offered at The Montessori Institute of San Diego, which may be of particular interest to special education teachers. Please note that the AMI Inclusive Education Course is open only to Montessori diploma holders at this time.[207]

After selecting an appropriate age group, or multiple age groups, look for a training center that best meets your educational

---

[204] Mosher, Rick. "Into the City: Near North Montessori School and the Uses of Environment." *The NAMTA Journal* 39.1 (2014): 112–27. Print.

[205] "Capacity." *AMI/USA*. AMI/USA, 2016. Web. 5 Oct. 2016. <http://ami-global.org/ami/what-is-ami/capacity>.

[206] "The NAMTA/AMI Montessori Orientation to Adolescent Studies (Ages 12-18)." *NAMTA*. North American Montessori Teachers' Association, 2016. Web. 5 Oct. 2016. <http://www.montessori-namta.org/The-AMI-Montessori-Orientation>.

[207] "Inclusive Education." *MISD Training Center*. The Montessori Institute of San Diego, 2016. Web. 18 Apr. 2018. <http://misdami.org/montessori-teacher-training-california/ami-montessori-courses/montessori-teacher-training-inclusive-education-certification-program/>.

needs. All AMI Montessori training courses, which are based upon oral tradition, are rigorous experiences that require at least 90% attendance, extensive note taking, reading selections, album making, hands-on practice with materials before, during, and after class, student observations, written exams, and an oral exam. You will be required to create "Montessori Albums," or lesson plan books, that are designed to help you facilitate student learning throughout your Montessori career. The number of Montessori Albums you will be required to create is dependent upon the course level you take. If you take Montessori Primary training, which lasts about nine months or three summers, you will be required to create five albums: Theory, Practical Life, Sensorial, Language, and Mathematics. You will also be required to write one or two "Theory Papers," which are similar to a thesis. There are also reading assignments. The Elementary course, which covers a six year age span, lasts approximately ten months and requires the submission of ten Montessori Albums related to theory and practice. If you are unable to take a sabbatical in order to receive Montessori training, a few training centers offer courses which can be taken over several summers rather than one school year. Some Montessori training centers also offer an option to simultaneously obtain a Master of Education through partner institutions such as Loyola University Maryland if this is a career path of interest. Keep these teacher training options in mind when selecting a Montessori training center.

Upon graduation from an AMI training center, you will receive a diploma from Association Montessori Internationale's world headquarters in Amsterdam, The Netherlands, which signifies your ability to lead a classroom in the age group you have studied. Unlike many types of teaching certificates, an AMI Diploma is an international document recognized by more than one hundred countries worldwide, and does not expire. While many public Montessori schools in America and around the world require a valid teaching license in addition to an AMI Diploma in order to legally teach, you can feel secure in the knowledge that your AMI Montessori training will never be regarded as an obsolete body of knowledge that requires expensive renewal fees at the end of some pre-determined time period. As for continuing education, your AMI Diploma will open the door to many exciting yet optional conferences and events that attract an international audience devoted to the same noble cause of child-centered education. You will also be eligible to attend exclusive "Refresher Courses," continuing education conferences open only to AMI Diploma holders. Like other Montessori conferences and events, Refresher Courses are optional but highly recommended. Many Montessori schools pay for their teachers to attend Montessori events, so be sure to ask your school district if Montessori continuing education experiences such as Refresher Courses can be included in the annual budget. In addition to continuing education opportunities, holding a Montessori diploma also makes you eligible to apply to the Inclusive Education Course offered at The Montessori Institute of San Diego. The Inclusive Education Course, which is held over two summers, may be of particular interest to teachers who wish to deepen their understanding of how Montessori education can optimally serve children with a variety of special needs including ADHD, autism, auditory impairments, visual impairments, long-term illnesses that require hospitalization, and giftedness to name a few.[208]

Montessori education in public school systems, while still a relatively rare phenomenon, is gradually expanding in response to changing community needs. It is clear that the traditional teacher-centered, one-size-fits-all, factory-based educational model designed in the 19th century is no longer appropriate for many students today in our rapidly changing 21st century. Our nation is no longer a land of assembly line factories but an economy of technological innovation.[209] In order to help prepare students for a

---

[208] Ibid.

world so different from that of their ancestors, many public schools are turning to Montessori as a means of fostering self-directed learning, independence, critical thinking, creativity, innovation,[210] and many other essential life skills.[211] The transition from Lockean model schooling to Montessori schooling is not one that will happen overnight, but the transition is gradually being implemented. As a public school teacher, you can prepare for the coming paradigm shift in education by investigating the Montessori Method and becoming trained in its unique philosophy and pedagogy. These are exciting times for the world of public schools. It is time to become prepared for the future.

References

"AMI Montessori and the Common Core State Standards." *AMI/USA*. AMI/USA, 2014. Web. 5 Oct. 2016. <https://amiusa.org/ami-montessori-and-the-common-core-state-standards/>.

"Capacity." *AMI/USA*. AMI/USA, 2016. Web. 5 Oct. 2016. <http://ami-global.org/ami/what-is-ami/capacity>.

"Desert Sky Montessori: Tuition-Free Montessori Elementary Education." *Desert Sky Montessori*. Desert Sky Montessori Charter School, 2018. Web. 4 Apr. 2018. <https://dsmontessori.org/>.

---

[209] Pofeldt, Elaine. "New Survey: Freelancers Now Make up 35% of US Workforce." *Forbes*. Forbes, Inc., 6 Oct. 2016. Web. 6 Oct. 2016. <http://www.forbes.com/sites/elainepofeldt/2016/10/06/new-survey-freelance-economy-shows-rapid-growth/#63c4547b737c.>

[210] McAfee, Andrew. "Montessori Builds Innovators." *Harvard Business Review*. Harvard Business Publishing, 25 July 2011. Web. 6 Oct. 2016. <https://hbr.org/2011/07/montessori-builds-innovators.>

[211] "Does It Work? What Research Says about Montessori and Student Outcomes." *National Center for Montessori in the Public Sector*. The National Center for Montessori in the Public Sector. Web. 6 Oct. 2016. <http://www.public-montessori.org/resources/does-it-work-what-research-says-about-montessori-and-student-outcomes.>

"Does It Work? What Research Says about Montessori and Student Outcomes." *National Center for Montessori in the Public Sector*. The National Center for Montessori in the Public Sector. Web. 6 Oct. 2016. <http://www.public-montessori.org/resources/does-it-work-what-research-says-about-montessori-and-student-outcomes>.

Einhorn, Erin. "Detroit Public Schools Try to Lure Skeptical Families by Adding Montessori Programs." *Chalkbeat*. Chalkbeat, 11 Aug. 2016. Web. 11 Aug. 2016. <http://www.chalkbeat.org/posts/detroit/2016/08/11/detroit-public-schools-try-lure-skeptical-families-adding-montessori-programs/>.

Fisicaro, Kailey. "Montessori Charter School Approved for Bend." *The Bulletin*. Bend, Oregon: A Western Communications Company, 28 Sept. 2016. Web. 28 Sept. 2016. <http://www.bendbulletin.com/localstate/education/4695067-151/montessori-charter-school-approved-for-bend>.

"Inclusive Education." *MISD Training Center*. The Montessori Institute of San Diego, 2016. Web. 18 Apr. 2018. <http://misdami.org/montessori-teacher-training-california/ami-montessori-courses/montessori-teacher-training-inclusive-education-certification-program/>.

McAfee, Andrew. "Montessori Builds Innovators." *Harvard Business Review*. Harvard Business Publishing, 25 July 2011. Web. 6 Oct. 2016. <https://hbr.org/2011/07/montessori-builds-innovators>.

"Montessori Program." Racine Unified School District, 2016. Web. 5 Oct. 2016. <http://www.rusd.org/montessori>.

Mosher, Rick. "Into the City: Near North Montessori School and the Uses of Environment." *The NAMTA Journal* 39.1 (2014): 112–27. Print.

"The NAMTA/AMI Montessori Orientation to Adolescent Studies (Ages 12-18)." *NAMTA*. North American Montessori Teachers' Association, 2016. Web. 5 Oct. 2016. <http://www.montessori-namta.org/The-AMI-Montessori-Orientation>.

"National Center for Montessori in the Public Sector." *National Center for Montessori in the Public Sector*. The National Center for Montessori in the Public Sector, 2018. Web. 4 Apr. 2018. <http://www.public-montessori.org/>.

Nielsen, Melinda, and AMI/USA. "The Three Essential Tools." *Montessori Guide*. Association Montessori Internationale of the United States, Inc., 2017. Web. 4 Apr. 2018. <http://montessoriguide.org/the-three-essential-tools/>.

"The Origins." *AMI/USA*. AMI/USA, 2014. Web. 3 Apr. 2018. <http://amiusa.org/the-origins/>.

Pofeldt, Elaine. "New Survey: Freelancers Now Make up 35% of US Workforce." *Forbes*. Forbes, Inc., 6 Oct. 2016. Web. 6 Oct. 2016. <http://www.forbes.com/sites/elainepofeldt/2016/10/06/new-survey-freelance-economy-shows-rapid-growth/#63c4547b737c>.

Ristow, Teresa. "First Day of School for Mountain Village Montessori." *Steamboat Today*. Steamboat Pilot & Today, 6 Sept. 2016. Web. 6 Sept. 2016. <http://www.steamboattoday.com/news/2016/sep/06/first-day-school-mountain-village-montessori/>.

Stocco, Nicholas. "Alder Montessori to Receive Preschool Promise Funding." *Montessori Northwest*. Montessori Northwest, 23 Sept. 2016. Web. 23 Sept. 2016. <http://montessori-nw.org/blog/alder-montessori-to-receive-preschool-promise-funding>.

"Training Courses." *Association Montessori Internationale*. Association Montessori Internationale, 2018. Web. 18 Apr. 2018. <https://montessori-ami.org/training-programmes/training-courses>.

MONTESSORI:
A GLOBAL MOVEMENT FOR PEACE

Introduction

When looking for an effective peace education movement on a global scale, look no further than the Montessori Method. Throughout its more than one hundred year history, Montessori has educated young children around the world in peaceful conflict resolution practices that facilitate negotiation and diplomacy. Often mistaken as an elitist method for the affluent,[212] Montessori education originally began as a program designed to serve low-income children in tenement housing.[213] Today, Montessori education for children of all ethnicities, social classes, and cultures has attracted increased interest due to its peaceful, child-centered philosophy and high academic standards[214] that have endured more than a century with worldwide success.[215] Most recently, a small but growing number of public school districts are beginning to establish new Montessori schools[216] or are converting existing traditional classrooms into Montessori prepared environments[217] in

---

[212] "Common Misconceptions." *NAMTA*. North American Montessori Teachers' Association, 2016 Web. 3 Apr. 2018. <http://www.montessori-namta.org/Common-Misconceptions>.

[213] "The National Center for Montessori in the Public Sector." *National Center for Montessori in the Public Sector*. American Montessori Society, 2016. Web. 5 Sept. 2016.< http://www.public-montessori.org/>.

[214] Lillard, Angeline. "Preschool Children's Development in Classic Montessori." *Journal of School Psychology* 50.3 (2012): 379–401. Print.

[215] "The Origins." *AMI/USA*. AMI/USA, 2014. Web. 5 Oct. 2016. <http://amiusa.org/the-origins/>.

[216] Manning, Rob. "Montessori Opens Preschool at Low-Income Oregon Elementary." *OPB*. Oregon Public Broadcasting, 2015. Web 1 Oct. 2016. <http://www.opb.org/news/article/montessori-opens-preschool-at-low-income-oregon-elementary/>.

[217] Thomas, Vickie. "DPS Incorporates Tuition-Free Montessori Programs into Some Schools." *CBS Local Media*. CBS Radio, Inc., 2016. Web. 13 July 2016.

response to community needs.[218] This is in addition to the numerous Montessori public charter schools that already exist throughout the country.[219]

Setting the Stage for Peace

Effective peace education is built into the Montessori curriculum starting on the first day of Primary school for children ages two-and-a-half through six. Rather than lecturing young children about getting along with one another, the Montessori teacher, known as a "guide," creates an ideal prepared environment that provides natural, intrinsic motivation for pro-social behavior. Readiness for peace begins with mutual respect between the students and the guide. At the beginning of each school day, the guide greets each child individually by name and shakes his hand. Following the morning greeting, children hang up their coats and put away their lunchboxes before choosing an activity. Note the phrase "choosing an activity." Integral to Montessori's peaceful, child-centered philosophy is the student's ability to independently choose any available activity in which he has previously received a lesson from the teacher. In Montessori, freely chosen educational activities are called "work." The term "work" does not connote drudgery. "Work" means that the child is engaged in a developmentally important task that is worthy of respect. Calling children's activities "work" affirms the importance of vital

---

<http://detroit.cbslocal.com/2016/07/13/dps-incorporates-tuition-free-montessori-programs-into-some-schools/>.

[218] Einhorn, Erin. "Detroit Public Schools Try to Lure Skeptical Families by Adding Montessori Programs." *Chalkbeat.* Chalkbeat, 2016. Web. 11 Aug. 2016. <http://www.chalkbeat.org/posts/detroit/2016/08/11/detroit-public-schools-try-lure-skeptical-families-adding-montessori-programs/#.V83XlElQ3IU>.

[219] "Public Montessori Schools in the United States." *National Center for Montessori in the Public Sector.* American Montessori Society, 2016. Web. 5 Sept. 2016. <http://public-montessori.org/census-project/schools-map>.

developmental tasks students perform throughout the day rather than the frivolous connotations which may be associated with the word "play." Even though the word "play" is not commonly associated with Montessori education, activities in the Montessori Primary classroom for two-and-a-half through six year old students are just as enjoyable as they are educational.[220] It is essential that children are free to independently choose their own work, after they have received a presentation with the material, in order to practice making decisions as a precursor to successful social relations including diplomacy. Good social skills and diplomacy require making choices about what words to use, what compromises to make, and what course of action should ultimately be taken. The Montessori Primary classroom prepares young children for these delicate social circumstances by allowing them to take an appropriate degree of responsibility for their educational activity choices.

Three Part Work Cycle

Primary children are further prepared for diplomacy and problem solving skills by following the three basic rules of the classroom beginning on the first day of school and continuing throughout their Montessori education:

1) A student may select any available material following an initial lesson from the teacher.

2) The student who has chosen an available material may work with it for as long as he desires during the classroom's minimum three hour uninterrupted work period.

---

[220] "The Prepared Environment." *NAMTA*. North American Montessori Teachers' Association, 2016. Web. 3 Apr. 2018. <http://www.montessori-namta.org/The-Prepared-Environment>.

3) When finished using a material, the student must return it to its proper location in the classroom in its original condition so it is ready for the next child to use.

These three rules, known as the "Three Part Work Cycle," provide an essential framework for student activities that simultaneously promotes spontaneous social order. The first rule, which states the student may select any available material following a lesson from the teacher, establishes clear boundaries regarding material use. If a material of interest is not currently on the shelf, it is unavailable. This typically means that another student is using the material, or that the teacher is giving a lesson using the material. Regardless of the reason, if a material is not available, the child may not choose it until it becomes available. This rule protects students' personal space, as a child may not take a material from another child who is using it as doing so would be disrespectful as well as a direct violation of the first rule of the classroom. Taking a material from another child is also a violation of the second rule of the classroom, which states that a student may work with a material until he is finished using it. This means that no other child may take the material away, nor may the teacher force the child to relinquish or share the material he is using. When the child using the material is finished and returns it to the shelf in its original condition, any child who has had a lesson may take a turn. This is better than forced sharing or artificial time limits on material use as these policies could cause resentment rather than peaceful social relations. The third rule of the classroom, which states that the student must return the material in its original condition, promotes respect for the material as well as thoughtful consideration for fellow students. Until the material is returned and ready for use, the child who wants to use the unavailable material must either wait his turn to use it or choose a different activity while waiting. This policy promotes problem solving skills and patience as the child who wants to use the unavailable material must decide independently what to do in the meantime while waiting. Problem solving and patience, integral components of diplomacy, are vital life skills which are naturally reinforced through the Montessori classroom's Three Part Work Cycle.

Grace and Courtesy

The Three Part Work Cycle alone is not sufficient preparation for optimal social skills. In addition to engaging in freely chosen educational activities, children in the Montessori Primary classroom learn manners, social graces, diplomacy, and safety through teacher-led presentations known as "Grace and Courtesy." During a Grace and Courtesy lesson, the guide invites a small group of three to seven children to watch her model a particular social skill such as saying "thank you," how to cough into a sleeve rather than into the air to help reduce the spread of disease, and respecting personal space. Once the group is settled, the guide models a specific skill in isolation. The guide then invites one student at a time to practice the modeled skill as presented. Following this practice period, the guide thanks the children for attending the presentation and then dismisses each child individually to choose other work. Over the next few days or weeks, the guide repeats each Grace and Courtesy lesson presented to several groups of three to seven students at a time. Grace and Courtesy lessons, like other presentations in the Montessori Primary classroom, are introduced and reviewed on an as-needed basis rather than by a set schedule. As students adopt and perfect the presented social skills, the guide introduces increasingly advanced Grace and Courtesy lessons including how to use diplomacy as a way to peaceably resolve conflicts.

The Peace Table

To help resolve conflicts between students in the Montessori Primary classroom, the guide introduces "The Peace Table." The Peace Table is a designated area in the classroom where two students who are having a dispute can meet to discuss their problems, take turns telling their sides of the story, express their feelings about the incident, and reach mutually beneficial solutions with minimal adult assistance. Typically, The Peace Table consists of a child-sized table, two child-sized chairs, and an object symbolic of peace that acts as an inanimate mediator. If two students are in the midst of a conflict, the guide gently intervenes and leads them over to The Peace Table to help them express their feelings in a constructive manner. The two children then sit across from one another at the table, if possible. Otherwise they may stand near the guide if they are too upset to formally use The Peace Table. Rather than taking sides in the argument, the guide demonstrates how to use The Peace Table's inanimate object as a mediator for the conflict. One child holds the object, such as a figurine of a globe or dove, and tells his side of the story. The other child listens without interrupting. When the first child is finished speaking, he transfers the object to the other child. It is now the second child's turn to speak without interruption. By taking turns telling their sides of the story and sharing their feelings about the situation with the help of the inanimate mediator, children receive an early, positive experience with the art of diplomacy. At first, taking turns holding the inanimate object generally requires assistance from the guide. Over time, as young children become more proficient at using The Peace Table and taking turns speaking, the guide's assistance is needed less frequently. The goal is for every child in the classroom to eventually be able to engage in peaceful conflict resolution at The Peace Table with minimal or no adult assistance.

Cultivating Peace

An official Montessori school, although ideal for many students, is not the only way to cultivate peace in young children. Peace begins with mutual respect between teachers and students. Every student, regardless of age, must be treated as a valued member of the home, classroom, and wider community. Establishing a foundation for mutual respect can begin with the teacher greeting each student individually by name when he enters the classroom. Give young children a prepared environment that allows them to make small choices throughout the day to help prevent tantrums, establish expectations, and foster a peaceful atmosphere. Examples of reasonable choices may include asking a child, "Would you like to wear the green hat or the brown hat today?" "Would you like to use crayons or colored pencils?" or "Would you like recycle the old newspaper now, or in five minutes?"

Model behavioral expectations and practice newfound skills through role play. Act out situations such as saying "excuse me," how to sneeze into a sleeve or tissue, or what to say if someone says something unkind. When working with children under six years of age, keep presentations brief and focus on one skill at a time. Children six years of age and older may enjoy being more involved in presentations such as helping to create a short, original skit to model social graces for their peers. Regardless of students' ages, a single lesson per skill is never enough to instill good manners. Like any other skill, repetition of Grace and Courtesy lessons is required for mastery.

Consider placing a Peace Table in your classroom or home as a place where children can peaceably solve conflicts when they arise. If children are in the midst of a conflict, make sure to listen respectfully to both sides of the story even if you saw what happened. Help students learn how to take turns holding an object symbolic of peace, such as a miniature globe, to peaceably resolve conflicts through respectful dialogue and empathy. Intervene when necessary to restore peace, but always strive toward fostering independent student use of The Peace Table to amicably resolve disputes.

Conclusion

With the multitude of violent conflicts afflicting the world today, it is now more important than ever to firmly establish peace education in early childhood. Thankfully, there is already an internationally recognized educational system in place to help create a more peaceful future. Montessori education, with its more than one hundred year history, may finally reach enough children worldwide to create a paradigm shift in the way adults view education and the way children grow up to view their world. As adults, there is only so much we can do to bring about lasting peace in these troubling times. Our job as educators is to create ideal conditions in which children are loved, respected, honored, and taught how to solve problems through Grace and Courtesy as well as diplomacy at The Peace Table. Once we have done this, the rest is up to the children. The world lies in their capable hands.

References

"Common Misconceptions." *NAMTA*. North American Montessori Teachers' Association, 2016 Web. 3 Apr. 2018. <http://www.montessori-namta.org/Common-Misconceptions>.

Einhorn, Erin. "Detroit Public Schools Try to Lure Skeptical Families by Adding Montessori Programs." *Chalkbeat*. Chalkbeat, 2016. Web. 11 Aug. 2016. <http://www.chalkbeat.org/posts/detroit/2016/08/11/detroit-public-schools-try-lure-skeptical-families-adding-montessori-programs/#.V83XlElQ3IU>.

Lillard, Angeline. "Preschool Children's Development in Classic Montessori." *Journal of School Psychology* 50.3 (2012): 379–401. Print.

Manning, Rob. "Montessori Opens Preschool at Low-Income Oregon Elementary." *OPB*. Oregon Public Broadcasting, 2015. Web 1 Oct. 2016. <http://www.opb.org/news/article/montessori-opens-preschool-at-low-income-oregon-elementary/>.

"Public Montessori Schools in the United States." *National Center for Montessori in the Public Sector*. American Montessori Society, 2016. Web. 5 Sept. 2016. <http://public-montessori.org/census-project/schools-map>.

"The National Center for Montessori in the Public Sector." *National Center for Montessori in the Public Sector*. American Montessori Society, 2016. Web. 5 Sept. 2016. <http://www.public-montessori.org/>.

"The Origins." *AMI/USA*. AMI/USA, 2014. Web. 3 Apr. 2018. <http://amiusa.org/the-origins/>.

"The Prepared Environment." *NAMTA*. North American Montessori Teachers' Association, 2016. Web. 5 Oct. 2016. <http://www.montessori-namta.org/The-Prepared-Environment>.

Thomas, Vickie. "DPS Incorporates Tuition-Free Montessori Programs into Some Schools." *CBS Local Media*. CBS Radio, Inc., 2016. Web. 13 July 2016. <http://detroit.cbslocal.com/2016/07/13/dps-incorporates-tuition-free-montessori-programs-into-some-schools/>.

Other Titles
by Mary Da Prato

Montessori for You and Your Child

Montessori Primary Terminology

Montessori Primary Addition

My First Montessori Book of Music Notation

My First Montessori Book of Leaf Shapes

My Montessori Coloring Book of Shapes

My First Montessori Book of Patterns

Thomas the Squirrel

The Peace Table

For a complete list of titles, visit the author's website at:
http://themontessorimysteryunveiled.weebly.com

Made in the USA
Columbia, SC
30 May 2021